COACHES GUIDE TO
TEACHING
SPORT SKILLS

ACEP Master Level Courses

ACEP Master Level courses are or will be available to accompany the following texts.

Sport Science

Coaches Guide to Sport Psychology by Rainer Martens discusses motivation, communication, leadership, and how to develop a variety of psychological skills.

Coaches Guide to Sport Physiology by Brian Sharkey leads coaches through the development of fitness-training programs suitable for their athletes.

Coaches Guide to Teaching Sport Skills by Robert Christina and Daniel Corcos uses practical examples to take coaches through the teaching/learning process.

Coaches Guide to Nutrition and Weight Control by Patricia Eisenman, Stephen Johnson, and Joan Benson provides practical guidelines to help coaches assist athletes in losing, gaining, or maintaining weight safely.

Coaches Guide to Social Issues in Sport by Jay Coakley and Robert Hughes examines how age, race, gender, and culture influence sport participation.

Coaches Guide to Sport Biomechanics describes the mechanical principles involved in sport movements.

Sports Medicine

Coaches Guide to Sport Injuries by J. David Bergeron and Holly Wilson Greene gives coaches information on injury prevention, emergency care, and follow-up procedures.

Coaches Guide to Sport Rehabilitation by Steven Tippett explains both the coach's role in rehabilitation and the process of rehabilitation as directed by health-care professionals.

Coaches Guide to Drugs and Sport examines the effects of a variety of abused drugs and the coach's role in combatting drug use.

Sport Management

Coaches Guide to Sport Law by Gary Nygaard and Thomas Boone explains the coach's legal duties in easy-to-understand terms.

Coaches Guide to Time Management by Charles Kozoll explains how to improve organization and avoid time-related stresses.

Coaches Guide to Sport Administration by Larry Leith provides guidelines to help coaches plan, organize, lead, and control their team's success.

Each course consists of a *Coaches Guide*, *Study Guide*, and *Workbook*. For more information, please contact

ACEP
Box 5076
Champaign, IL 61825-5076
1-800-747-4457

COACHES GUIDE TO TEACHING SPORT SKILLS

A publication for the
American Coaching Effectiveness Program
Master Level Sport Science Curriculum

Robert W. Christina, PhD
Penn State University

Daniel M. Corcos, PhD
University of Illinois at Chicago

HUMAN KINETICS BOOKS
Champaign, Illinois

Library of Congress Cataloging-in-Publication Data

Christina, Robert W.
    Coaches guide to teaching sport skills / Robert W. Christina,
Daniel M. Corcos.
        p. cm.

    "A publication for the American Coaching Effectiveness Program,
level 2 sport science curriculum."
    Bibliography: p.
    Includes index.
    ISBN 0-87322-020-X
    1. Coaching (Athletics) 2. Physical education and training—Study
and teaching—United States. I. Corcos, Daniel M., 1954-   .
II. American Coaching Effectiveness Program. III. Title.
GV711.C52 1988   87-19687
796'.07'7—dc 19   CIP

Developmental Editor: Linda Anne Bump, PhD
Copy Editor: Patrick O'Hayer
Assistant Editor: JoAnne Cline
Production Director: Ernie Noa
Projects Manager: Lezli Harris
Typesetter: Theresa Bear
Text Design: Keith Blomberg
Cartoon Illustrations: Jerry Barrett
Cover Design and Layout: Jack Davis
Printed By: Versa Press

ISBN: 0-87322-020-X
Copyright © 1988 by Robert W. Christina and Daniel M. Corcos

Printed in the United States of America

10 9 8 7 6 5 4

Human Kinetics Books
A Division of Human Kinetics Publishers
Box 5076
Champaign, IL 61825-5076
1-800-747-4457

Canada Office:
Human Kinetics Publishers
P.O. Box 2503, Windsor, ON N8Y 4S2
1-800-465-7301 (in Canada only)

Europe Office:
Human Kinetics Publishers (Europe) Ltd.
P.O. Box IW14
Leeds LS16 6TR
England
0532-781708

Australia Office:
Human Kinetics Publishers
P.O. Box 80
Kingswood 5062
South Australia
374-0433

Dedication

To my wife Barbara and to our children Bob, Lynn, and Lori. (RWC)

To Kathleen, Caroline, and Amanda, Hildegard and Basil, Alison and Edward. (DMC)

Acknowledgments

We would like to express our sincere appreciation to Dr. Rainer Martens who served as a constant source of encouragement and support in our efforts to complete this book. We also would like to acknowledge the substantial contribution made by Drs. Linda Bump and Steve Jefferies to the organization and writing of this book. In fact, the assistance of the entire Human Kinetics staff, who provided us with many insightful suggestions for improving the clarity of the book, is greatly appreciated.

As most of us know, coaches make an enormous contribution to the lives of their athletes both on and off the field, as do teachers both in and out of the classroom. Many of the ideas expressed in this book came from Bob Dean and James "Bucky" Freeman, two coaches of the first author, and Alec Thom and Tommy Johnson, two coaches of the second author. Other ideas for which we are very grateful came from Martin Underwood, David Edgecombe, Tom Carstens, Drs. Jack Adler, Michael Ellis, Marjorie Woollacott, Steven Keele, and Peter Travers. The authors also would like to thank Drs. Karl Newell, Michael Wade, Bryant Cratty, Daniel Landers, Rainer Martens, Mary Ann Roberton, Lolas Halverson, and Douglas Larish for providing much valuable material. A very special thanks is extended to Dr. Roy Clumpner, Susan Hagmeier, Dr. Don Hellison, Michael Peterson, Dr. Maureen Weiss, and Dr. Gary Wiren for their insightful comments on earlier versions of the book.

The first author would like to acknowledge all of the former athletes, about 300 of them, who played on teams he coached in five different sports. Many of the ideas expressed in this book emanated from working with these athletes. Many others came from involvement with coaching education programs conducted by the U.S. Olympic Committee and national sports governing bodies such as the U.S. Shooting Team, National Rifle Association, USA Wrestling, U.S. Ski Coaches Association, U.S. Diving Association, U.S. Equestrian Team, and U.S. Field Hockey Association.

Finally to Mrs. Pat McMullen, who spent many hours first trying to read my writing and then typing the different versions and revisions of this book, one big "thanks" from the first author. The second author would like to extend a special thanks to Drs. Gerry Gottlieb and Richard Penn who provided him with the time and facilities to coauthor this book.

Contents

Introduction

The *Coaches Guide to Teaching Sport Skills* is one of a series of sport science texts selected for inclusion in the Master Level of the American Coaching Effectiveness Program (ACEP). ACEP is designed to help coaches like you make their programs a valuable and enjoyable experience for their athletes. The Master Level has been written for teachers and coaches who are interested in learning more about the sport sciences, sports medicine, and sport management.

OBJECTIVES

The main purpose of this book is to help you improve the way you teach sports skills. Whether you coach skilled players or beginners, whether you have coached for few or many years, knowing how to teach skills effectively is one of your primary responsibilities as a coach. You may be teaching new skills to beginning athletes or suggesting refinements to advanced players who never learned certain fundamental techniques correctly. Even very advanced players have weaknesses in certain facets of their skill technique that can be overcome by systematic instruction.

This book provides you with information about teaching and learning skills that is applicable to many different sports. Many practical examples are included to show you how this information can be applied. We have provided examples of application to different skill levels and age groups. This book is primarily written for coaches of athletes between 6 and the late teen years, but much information will benefit you regardless of the age group you coach.

Although we will provide information to guide you in teaching sport skills, what may work for one sport or one team may not work for another. A football quarterback needs to learn how to monitor many events happening at once so that he can select the best play out of many options; on the other hand, a golfer needs to be taught to focus on just one event and eliminate all other distractions. Consequently, few hard and fast rules exist for you to follow. You will have to apply what you learn to your sport and your athletes. Although we have made some recommendations that might appear to be somewhat inflexible, this is not the intent. These recommendations are given so you will have some specific guidelines with which to begin. As you test them and become more experienced, you will learn how to adapt them to fit your coaching situation.

YOUR RESPONSIBILITY TO YOUR ATHLETES

In this book, you will learn how to become a better coach by becoming a better teacher of sport skills. Apart from teaching sport skills, as an educator you have an obligation to your athletes not only as athletes, but as youngsters who have many other potential abilities, talents, and interests that should be allowed to develop. Early specialization in one sport may lead to a high level of skill proficiency, but it will not allow young athletes to develop a variety of physical abilities and talents or to find the ones in which they are most gifted. Furthermore, early specialization may provide such a restricted environment for young athletes that they do not realize some aspects of their social and emotional development.

Another problem with specialization lies in an athlete's position on a team (e.g., center in basketball, goalkeeper in soccer) and the types of skills you teach (e.g., tackling as opposed to dribbling the ball in soccer). These factors may not be the most appropriate skills for the athlete's optimum performance in later life. Because children all grow at different rates (most dramatic in girls between the ages of 10 and 14 and in boys between 12 and 15), coaches often take advantage of athletes who mature early by playing them in positions where they can best use their physical attributes. Consequently, these children do not develop all the skills required for the sport and suffer when the other children catch up with them. For example, a physically large, strong football player who matures early can often cover a lot of ground by running in a straight line without needing to learn how to change pace, side step, or feint. In high school and college, his contemporaries who mature later may be better players because they did not have the strength to simply run through the opposition, requiring them to learn other strategies. Handling these situations is often very difficult because one sure way to win in many sports is to always give the ball to your biggest athlete.

On the other hand, athletes who mature late are often abused by the sporting community. These athletes often get cut from the team, have to sit on the bench, get little playing time, or play in nonessential positions. Sensitive coaching requires both unselfishness and the ability to explain the reasons underlying your coaching decisions to your athletes and to their parents. *Remember that as a coach you are first and foremost an educator whose primary mission is to help each of your athletes become all that he or she can become not only in sport but in life.*

ORGANIZATION OF THE BOOK

This book has been divided into four parts. Part 1 will prepare you to teach sport skills. In chapter 1 you will learn about all of your major instructional responsibilities for a single season, including what you need to do before, during, and after the season to make your instructional program as effective as possible.

But this is only part of what you need to know before you actually begin teaching skills. The other part, covered in chapter 2, involves understanding the skill learning process so that you will be ready to adjust your teaching relative to the learning needs of your athletes.

Part 2 will tell you how to present sport skills that you want your athletes to learn. In chapters 3 and 4 you will learn how to introduce, explain, and demonstrate skills effectively. If your athletes are able to perform the skill you present, they can begin practicing it. However, if they cannot perform the skill well enough to begin practicing it, you will have to help them. Chapter 5 explains how you can do this.

Part 3 will focus on how you can get your athletes to develop and maintain the skills you present. Chapter 6 will discuss practice and the variables that influence the effectiveness of practice in developing and maintaining skills. In chapter 7 we will help you to make complex skills easier for your athletes to learn. The use of feedback, one of the most powerful variables in developing and maintaining skills, is presented in chapter 8. And, in chapter 9 you will learn how to effectively analyze your athletes' skill performance and to use a positive approach to correct their errors.

Part 4 will discuss four cognitive processes important in the performance of sport skills. In chapters 10 and 11 you will learn how imagery and memory are involved in sport skills. Attention and how to get your athletes to focus their attention will be presented in chapter 12. Finally, chapter 13 focuses on how to help your athletes anticipate and respond quickly.

We hope the four parts of this book contribute to your success as a coach by helping you become a more effective teacher of sport skills. Don't keep your athletes waiting any longer! They need your help and this book will tell you how you can give it to them. So get started and good luck!

PART I
Preparing to Teach Skills

Teaching sport skills effectively requires advanced instructional planning and an understanding of the skill learning process in relation to the instructional process. In the first part of this book you will learn about what you need to do and know before you actually begin to teach. Chapter 1 will focus on your instructional responsibilities before, during, and after a single season. It will help you plan in advance to meet the goals you have set. You'll plan what to teach, how to teach it, when to teach it, and how to determine if the goal was achieved. Chapter 2 will tell you about the skill learning process and the stages your athletes go through as they develop skills. You will find out what to look for as your athletes learn skills. Identifying correct aspects of skills is invaluable in helping you to individualize your instruction and adjust your teaching to the learning needs of each of your athletes.

Chapter 1
Knowing Your Instructional Responsibilities

This chapter presents a systematic framework of progressive steps you should follow when teaching sport skills. The material is adapted from the instructional information presented in the American Coaching Effectiveness Program (ACEP) text *Coaching Young Athletes* (Martens, Christina, Harvey, & Sharkey, 1981). These steps will help you incorporate teaching and learning theory in your coaching. Figure 1.1 illustrates the seven-step system of major instructional responsibilities that you must carry out before, during, and after a typical season.

PRESEASON INSTRUCTIONAL PLANNING RESPONSIBILITIES

Preseason instructional planning comprises the first four steps shown in Figure 1.1: establishing instructional goals, selecting subject matter, organizing material, and evaluating initial skills. If you have read *Coaching Young Athletes* (Martens et al., 1981), you will already be familiar with some of these steps. However, in this book we will examine your instructional responsibilities in greater detail.

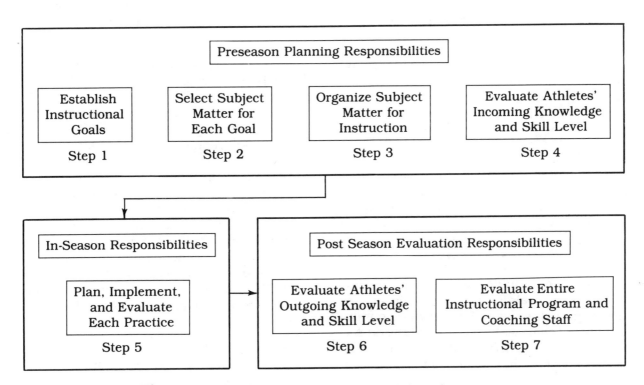

Figure 1.1 Coach's instructional responsibilities for a season.

Step 1: Establish Instructional Goals

Instructional goals are general statements of what you expect your athletes to have learned by the end of the season, and they should be written so that you will be able to verify whether or not your athletes have achieved them. Each of your goals should clearly meet the following three criteria:

- State the *performance* in observable and measurable terms.
- State the *conditions* under which the performance is to occur.
- Indicate the *standard* upon which goal attainment can be evaluated.

The following two examples of instructional goals meet these criteria.

"The wrestlers will be able to demonstrate that they have mastered the fundamental skills necessary to participate successfully in practice and team matches at a novice level."

- *Performance* = demonstrate mastery of the fundamental skills.
- *Conditions* = in practice and team matches.
- *Standard* = mastered skills necessary to participate successfully at a novice level.

"The soccer players will be able to display accurate and complete knowledge of the basic rules of the game through their play in practice and game situations throughout the entire season."

- Performance = display knowledge of the basic rules through their play.
- *Conditions* = in practice and game situations.
- *Standard* = accurate and complete throughout the entire season.

After you have established your instructional goals for the season, you should use them in three ways. First, review your instructional goals with your team at the outset of the season and periodically thereafter. It is important that they understand what you want them to accomplish. Second, distribute the goals to parents, assistant coaches, and others interested in your program so that they also know what you are trying to achieve. Finally, use them as a basis for the next step, selecting the subject matter for instruction.

Step 2: Select the Subject Matter for Each Goal

The subject matter you select will depend on your instructional goals and will typically include information, sport skills and strategies, and sportsmanship behaviors. Ask yourself, What will the athletes need to learn to achieve this specific instructional goal? The answer will be a list of skills, information, and behaviors they will need to learn to achieve the goal, and will constitute the subject matter you will present. Tables 1.1, 1.2, and 1.3 are examples of such lists for a wrestling program concerning, respectively, skills, nutrition and weight control knowledge, and sportsmanship behavior.

After you have composed your list for each instructional goal, use the following checklist to evaluate the subject matter you selected.

Subject Matter Checklist
- [ ] Is the skill reasonably safe?
- [ ] Do the athletes have the physical strength to perform the skill?
- [ ] Do the athletes have sufficient motor coordination to begin learning the skill?
- [ ] If the skill requires lead-up skill training, have the athletes mastered those skills?
- [ ] Does your subject matter contribute to the instructional goal more effectively than other possible choices?
- [ ] Are the athletes interested in learning the subject matter? If not, can enthusiasm for learning it be generated at this level?
- [ ] Is the subject matter accurate?
- [ ] Do the athletes have sufficient emotional and intellectual maturity to begin learning the subject matter?

If the answer to any of these questions is *no*, replace or eliminate that item from the list.

Step 3: Organize the Subject Matter for Instruction

Once you have selected the subject matter to achieve your instructional goals, you need to organize it into a tentative instructional schedule, or master plan, for the season. A complete instructional schedule that includes all of the subject matter you selected in Step 2 will help you provide continuity in planning from one practice to the next.

Table 1.1
Individual Skills Selected to Achieve Wrestling Goal 1*

Goal 1
The wrestlers will be able to demonstrate they have mastered the fundamental wrestling skills necessary to successfully participate in practices and matches at a novice level.

Individual Skills

Takedowns
1. Dos and don'ts
2. Tie ups
3. Double leg
4. Single leg
5. Arm drag
6. Fireman's carry
7. Duck under

Escapes and Reversals
1. Referee's starting position
2. Dos and don'ts
3. Stand up
4. Sit back, turn in
5. Hip roll
6. Switch

Breakdowns and Rides
1. Dos and don'ts
2. Cross face-near leg
3. Far ankle-waist
4. Two-on-one ride

Pinning Combinations
1. Half nelson
2. Cross face cradle
3. Arm bar-reverse half
4. Three-quarter nelson

Counters to Takedowns
1. Defense on your feet
2. Hip block
3. Whizzer
4. Cross face
5. Quarter nelson
6. Pancake

Counters to Escapes and Reversals
1. Counter to stand up
2. Counter to sit back, turn in
3. Counter to hip roll
4. Counter to switch

Counters to Breakdowns and Rides
1. Counter to cross face-near leg
2. Counter to ankle-knee bump
3. Counter to far ankle-waist
4. Counter to two-on-one ride

Counters to Pinning Combinations
1. Regaining a base
2. Counter to half nelson
3. Counter to arm bar
4. Counter to cradle
5. Counter to three-quarter nelson

---

*From *Coaching Young Athletes* (p. 78) by R. Martens, R. W. Christina, J. S. Harvey, Jr., and B. J. Sharkey, 1981, Champaign, IL: Human Kinetics. Copyright 1981 by Rainer Martens, Robert W. Christina, John S. Harvey, Jr., and Brian J. Sharkey. Adapted by permission.

Table 1.4 is an example of how to organize instruction and practice for teaching the skills selected to achieve the first wrestling goal (see Table 1.1). This is a tentative instructional schedule for the season based on two practices a week. In this example, the schedule of skills to be taught (T) and practiced (P) at each session forms a systematic instructional sequence, indicating what to teach and practice as well as when to do so. When considering instructional goals that involve knowledge and behaviors, you should list what you would like to cover (see Table 1.2 and 1.3) and use these lists as a basis for planning practices.

Table 1.2
Nutrition and Weight Control Knowledge Selected to Achieve Wrestling Goal 2*

Goal 2
The wrestlers will be able to demonstrate knowledge of proper nutrional and safe weight control practices and be able to apply it to themselves.

—— **Nutrition and Weight Control** ——

Nutrition and Diet
1. Need for proper nutrition
2. Elements of a balanced diet
   - Milk group
   - Meat group
   - Vegetable-fruit group
   - Bread-cereal group
3. Meal composition and performance
   - Carbohydrates
   - Fats
   - Proteins
   - Sugars
   - Vitamins
   - Minerals
4. Size and timing of meals relative to exercise or competition
   - Pre- and postpractice
   - Pre- and postmatch
   - Tournament
5. The need for water
   - Water as bodybuilding material
   - Water as a regulator of body processes
6. Use of drugs and their effect on health and performance
   - Coffee
   - Tea
   - Alcohol
   - Smoking
   - Other drugs

Optimum Body Weight
1. How to estimate it
   - Age
   - Body surface area
   - Growth level
   - Amount of physical activity
2. How to achieve it and maintain it over a season
   - Balanced diet
   - Proper amount of physical activity
3. Discourage the practice of fluid deprivation and dehydration to "make weight"
   - Rubber suits
   - Steam rooms
   - Saunas
   - Hot boxes
   - Laxatives
   - Diuretics
4. Physiological consequences and medical complications resulting from fluid deprivation, dehydration, and food restriction

---

From *Coaching Young Athletes* (p. 79) by R. Martens, R. W. Christina, J. S. Harvey, Jr., and B. J. Sharkey, 1981, Champaign, IL: Human Kinetics. Copyright 1981 by Rainer Martens, Robert W. Christina, John S. Harvey, Jr., and Brian J. Sharkey. Adapted by permission.

Table 1.3
Sportsmanship Behaviors Selected to Achieve Wrestling Goal 3*

Goal 3
The wrestlers will be able to demonstrate appropriate sportsmanship behaviors in practices and matches.

Sportsmanship Behaviors

1. Demonstrates proper control of emotions.
2. Demonstrates use of appropriate language.
3. Is courteous to opponents, teammates, officials, coaches, and parents.
4. Is humble in winning and gracious in defeat.
5. Respects opponent as a person in winning and losing.
6. Abides by the rules of wrestling and never intentionally uses questionable holds or attempts to punish an opponent.

*From *Coaching Young Athletes* (p. 81) by R. Martens, R. W. Christina, J. S. Harvey, Jr., and B. J. Sharkey, 1981, Champaign, IL: Human Kinetics. Copyright 1981 by Rainer Martens, Robert W. Christina, John S. Harvey, Jr., and Brian J. Sharkey. Adapted by permission.

Table 1.4
Partial Instructional Schedule for Wrestling Goal 1*

Goal 1
The wrestlers will be able to demonstrate they have mastered the fundamental wrestling skills necessary to successfully participate in practices and matches at a novice level.

Skills	Month 1 Week 1 T	Week 1 Th	Week 2 T	Week 2 Th	Week 3 T	Week 3 Th	Week 4 T	Week 4 Th	Month 2 Week 1 T	Week 1 Th	Week 2 T	Week 2 Th	...etc.	Time (in minutes) spent on each skill for the season
Takedowns														
1. Dos & don'ts	T(10)	P(10)	P(5)						P(5)					30
2. Tie ups	T(15)	P(10)	P(10)	P(10)					P(10)					55
3. Double leg			T(15)	P(15)	P(10)			P(10)	P(10)		P(10)			70
4. Single leg						T(15)	P(15)	P(10)	P(10)		P(10)			60
(etc.)													Total Time	215
Counters to Takedowns														
1. Defense on feet	T(15)	P(10)	P(5)					P(10)						40
2. Hip block								T(15)	P(10)	P(10)				35
3. Whizzer									T(10)	P(10)				20
4. Cross face										T(10)	P(10)			20
(etc.)													Total Time	115
Escapes and Reversals														
1. Referee's starting position	T(10)		P(5)											15
2. Dos & don'ts	T(10)		P(5)	P(5)					P(5)					25
3. Stand up	T(10)		P(15)	P(10)	P(10)		P(10)				P(10)			65
4. Switch					T(15)	P(15)	P(10)				P(10)			50
(etc.)													Total Time	155

Note: T(10) = Teach skill for the first time for 10 minutes.

P(10) = Practice or drill the skill as a team for 10 minutes.

As the season progresses, individual practice time should be built into your instructional schedule so that your athletes can practice what they would like.

*From *Coaching Young Athletes* (p. 88) by R. Martens, R.W. Christina, J.S. Harvey, Jr., and B.J. Sharkey, 1981, Champaign, IL: Human Kinetics. Copyright 1981 by Rainer Martens, Robert W. Christina, John S. Harvey, Jr., and Brian J. Sharkey. Adapted by permission.

To develop a tentative instructional schedule, begin by ordering the skills within each category; list the basic skills first and the most complex skills last. This will determine the order in which to teach these skills. In Table 1.4, for example, under the category Escapes and Reversals, *referee's starting position* and *do's and don'ts* are the basic skills that should be taught before the *stand up*. In addition, the instructional schedule should include the amount of time you plan to spend on each skill (a) at each practice session, (b) for each week, (c) for each month, and (d) for the entire season.

The instructional schedule is not intended to be a rigid format that ignores the individual learning rates of your athletes or their personal learning goals. You should think of it, rather, as a tentative master plan that will very likely have to be adjusted several times throughout the season to reflect your athlete's progress. The following suggestions will assist you in maintaining an appropriate level of flexibility in your instructional schedule.

- Schedule a certain amount of time at each practice session for your athletes to practice the skills of their choice.
- Change your instructional schedule anytime the athletes are not progressing as planned or the schedule is not meeting the needs of your athletes.
- Don't expect all your athletes to learn all the skills listed in your schedule. An individual's existing skill level and ability to learn new skills will affect the number of skills he or she can master.

If you are a veteran coach working with a group of athletes you already know, you should be able to put together a tentative instructional schedule that will require few adjustments during the season. If you are relatively new to coaching, you can benefit from the advice of more experienced coaches and physical education teachers; consulting them should be helpful to you in initially constructing a realistic schedule. However, accurately predicting the amount of time needed to teach the various sport skills will be quite difficult if you are new to coaching, cannot consult experienced colleagues, and are working with a group of athletes unfamiliar to you. If this is the case, you might benefit from constructing plans to cover shorter periods, such as 1 to 2 weeks, rather than outlining practice times for the entire season. This approach should make it easier to modify the schedule if you aren't moving at the predicted rate.

Creating a tentative instructional schedule requires a great deal of work. However, once you have written, tested, and revised it, you will probably not have to make many major changes in it for future seasons. Thus, it will save you considerable planning time in the long run.

Step 4: Evaluate Athletes' Incoming Knowledge and Skill Level

After organizing the subject matter for instruction, you should evaluate your athletes' preseason knowledge and skill level in relation to the subject matter selected. This can be done during the first few practices by using either the team evaluation form (see Figure 1.2) or a form of your own design. Whatever form you use should list the subject matter in the same order as it appears in your instructional schedule. For example, the order of the skills listed in Figure 1.2 follows the same sequence as that shown in the partial instructional schedule in Table 1.4.

Perhaps the best way to conduct your evaluation is to begin with the simplest subject matter and proceed toward the more complex. Have the athletes identify the items listed on your evaluation form that they know or are capable of performing. If someone claims to understand a rule or strategy or to be able to perform a skill (e.g., double-leg takedown), ask the athlete to demonstrate his or her level of competency and evaluate it on the form.

A word of caution: Some skills are more dangerous to perform than others—especially during the preseason, when athletes have not been practicing and may not be in the best physical condition. You will have to use judgment; if a skill seems too difficult to perform safely during your preseason evaluation, exclude it from competency testing. Most important, if your athletes have not claimed competency for a skill or you have given no formal, systematic instruction in the skill, never ask them to perform it.

When your evaluation is complete you will have a good idea of your athletes' competency in terms of your instructional goals and your

Date _____	Names of Athletes	Team Average for Each Skill

Skills

Takedowns
1. Dos and don'ts
2. Tie ups
3. Double leg
4. Single leg
5. Arm drag
6. Fireman's carry
7. Duck under

Counters to takedowns
1. Defense on your feet
2. Hip block
3. Whizzer
4. Cross face
5. Quarter nelson
6. Pancake

Escapes and reversals
1. Referee's starting position
2. Dos and don'ts
3. Stand up
4. Switch
.
.
.
etc.

Performance Evaluation Categories

1 = Unable to perform
2 = Below average
3 = Average
4 = Above average
NA = Not applicable

Figure 1.2   Sample team evaluation form.

instructional schedule. This information will help you individualize your instruction because you will be able to select the subject matter (e.g., knowledge, skills, etc.) that is most appropriate for each of your athletes to learn and practice. You must begin your instruction according to the performance level of the athletes. Starting below their level is unnecessary and can lead to boredom and discipline problems, and starting too far above their level is frustrating, discouraging, and potentially unsafe. Your ability to evaluate the knowledge and skill level of your athletes is

one of the cornerstones for establishing rapport with the team.

We also recommend that you transfer the information from the team evaluation form to an athlete evaluation form (see Figure 1.3) and give each athlete his or her own copy. Distribute the forms at one of the first practices of the season immediately after you have discussed your instructional goals with your athletes, as recommended in Step 1. Review the athlete evaluation form with the team as a whole and encourage each athlete to set his or her own personal learning goals within the framework of the skills listed on the form. Tell the athletes to identify the skills they'd like to learn and to set their personal learning goals slightly above the level of their evaluations. If you encourage them to review these goals regularly they will realize their accomplishments and experience the success that is essential for steady learning progress. Be certain to point out that it may not be possible for everyone to achieve all of the instructional goals and to learn every skill listed on the form, although you would like them to do so. Tell the group what is most important is that each athlete should strive to achieve the goals that he or she has set out to achieve.

Incidentally, the team and athlete evaluation need not be limited only to preseason and

postseason use. We encourage you to review them from time to time during the season to enable you to track your athletes' progress according to your instructional schedule. This will let you know how much your athletes have learned between the beginning of the season and your first in-season evaluation and between then and your second in-season evaluation. It also will tell you what your athletes still need to master by the season's end.

Use this information to help you modify your instructional schedule and teaching in relation to your athletes' progress. Discussing the evaluation with your athletes individually allows you to alert each one to his or her progress or lack of it since the beginning of the season. The athletes will gain a sense of

Athlete's Name _____ Coach _____ Date _____ Skills _____	Preseason Evaluation	Athlete's Goals	Midseason Evaluation	Postseason Evaluation	Comments
Takedowns 1. Dos and don'ts 2. Tie ups 3. Double leg 4. Single leg 5. Arm drag 6. Fireman's carry 7. Duck under					
Counters to takedowns 1. Defense on your feet 2. Hip block 3. Whizzer 4. Cross face 5. Quarter nelson 6. Pancake					
Escapes and reversals 1. Referee's starting position 2. Dos and don'ts 3. Stand up 4. Switch . . . etc.					

Performance Evaluation Categories

1 = Unable to execute   4 = Above average
2 = Below average   NA = Not applicable
3 = Average

Figure 1.3 Sample athlete evaluation form.

accomplishment from these reviews, and their motivation to learn is likely to increase.

IN-SEASON INSTRUCTIONAL RESPONSIBILITIES

Among all the major steps presented in Figure 1.1, fulfilling your responsibilities for each practice during the season is critical for effective coaching. This step is so important, in fact, that most of the rest of this book is devoted to it.

Step 5: Plan, Implement, and Evaluate Each Practice

At this stage you will be choosing subject matter to teach, review, and refine for *each* practice. You should begin by reviewing your instructional schedule to determine what you had planned to cover in the practice and the amount of time you had allocated to it. You must take into account the progress your athletes have made in previous practices and assess what they've actually learned in comparison with your instructional schedule projections of what they would have learned by this time in the season. Also, consider input from the athletes and assistant coaches and be aware of the amount of practice time you have available. You need to accommodate all of these factors in selecting your subject matter for the day's practice.

Instructional Method

Knowing *how* to teach is just as important as knowing *what* to teach. Once you select the subject matter, you will need to choose your instructional methods. This process involves many instructional decisions:

- Will the skill be taught by the *whole* or *part* method?
- What instructional materials and devices will be needed to teach and practice the skill effectively (e.g., videotape, mirror, soccer kick board, baseball batting tees, blocking dummies for football)?
- How will the skill be introduced and explained?
- How will the skill be demonstrated and who will demonstrate it?

- What will you do if all or most of your athletes are unable to perform the skill after being taught?
- How will the skill be practiced after being taught?
- How will you use feedback during practice to provide information, reinforcement, motivation, and, if necessary, punishment?
- How will you analyze your athletes' performance as they practice and effectively make corrections?

These are a few examples of the types of decisions that must be made before each upcoming practice and that significantly impact teaching effectiveness. Chapters 3 through 13 present information that will help you make instructional decisions and select methods.

The Practice Area

Remember that you will need to prepare the practice area for what you plan to teach and how you plan to teach it. For example, if you are teaching youngsters how to dribble a basketball or soccer ball through a complex pattern, you should plan to set up the obstacle course prior to practice. If you are teaching tennis players how to improve the accuracy of their shots using targets on a wall, you will need to mark different areas of the wall before practice begins. Try to avoid keeping your players waiting while you complete organizational steps that you could have taken care of before they arrived. You will find other specific examples of instructional methods in chapters 3 through 13.

Designing a Practice Plan

Figure 1.4 is a sample practice plan for a 1½-hour session and should serve as a general guide to help you design your own practice plans. The following sections examine each of the key elements of this example.

Date.   The first step is to record the date so that you know when you taught the session. This will help you after the season when you are evaluating and revising your instructional schedule in preparation for the following season.

Performance Objectives.   You should write performance objectives for each practice.

Date:
Performance objectives:
Equipment:
Time schedule and parts of practice:*
    4:00-4:10 Warm-up
    4:10-4:30 Practice previously taught skills
    4:30-4:55 Teach and practice new skills
    4:55-5:20 Practice under competitive conditions
    5:20-5:25 Cool-down
    5:25-5:30 Coach's comments
Evaluation of the practice:

*These are sample times. Feel free to adjust them
to fit your schedule.

Figure 1.4   Sample outline for a practice.

These objectives should be specific statements of what you want your athletes to know or be able to do as a result of a particular practice session. *Do not confuse performance objectives with instructional goals.* Instructional goals are general statements of what the athletes should know or be able to do as a result of your coaching over the course of the entire season. A performance objective is more specific than an instructional goal.

Your performance objectives will come from your instructional schedule. The objectives you select for a particular practice session will be indicated by your instructional schedule. Let's use Table 1.4 as an example. If it is Tuesday of Week 3 of Month 1, your performance objectives should focus on teaching the switch for the first time and practicing two previously taught skills, the stand up and the double-leg takedown.

Write performance objectives as you would instructional goals, but much more specifically. They should identify

- the *performance* stated in observable and measurable terms,

- the *conditions* under which the performance is to occur, and
- the *standard* stating when the objective is achieved.

Examples of performance objectives are:
"The athletes will be able to perform a throw-in three consecutive times according to the rules of soccer during the throw-in drill in practice."

- *Performance* = perform a throw-in.
- *Conditions* = during the throw-in drill in practice.
- Standard = three consecutive times according to the rules of soccer.

"The athletes will be able to perform a lay-up shot that goes in the basket at least 7 times out of 10 attempts with their nondominant hand during the lay-up drill in basketball practice."

- *Performance* = perform a lay-up shot with nondominant hand.
- *Conditions* = during the lay-up drill in basketball practice.
- *Standard* = that goes in the basket at least 7 times in 10 attempts.

"The athletes will be able to execute a sacrifice bunt that is a fair ball and rolls on the ground at least 4 times out of 6 attempts during the bunting drill in baseball practice."

- *Performance* = execute a sacrifice bunt.
- Condition = during the bunting drill in baseball practice.
- *Standard* = that is a fair ball and rolls on the ground at least 4 times out of 6 attempts.

Equipment. List the equipment (e.g., mats, balls, bats) needed to conduct practice. Make sure that the equipment you plan to use is safe, clean, and operational before you begin and remember to bring it to practice.

Time Schedule. A time schedule will help you make efficient use of your time. Without one, it's easy to spend too much time on one skill and fail to accomplish much of what you had set out to do. You should not, of course, be afraid to adjust the schedule as practice proceeds. Your athletes may need more practice time than you originally allocated to master a difficult skill, or you may decide that a change of pace is needed to recapture the athletes' interest and attention. Plan carefully and specifically but be flexible.

The time schedule in the sample plan is fairly typical but can be varied according to how much time you want to spend on a particular part of the practice. The usual parts of a practice session and the order in which they typically occur are also shown in this plan. Although you occasionally may not use all of these parts or may decide to vary the order shown, you should follow these recommendations most of the time.

Warm-up. Every practice should begin with appropriate warm-up exercises. The importance of warming up cannot be overemphasized. Athletes need to prepare for practice physiologically and psychologically. Failure to warm up adequately will increase the risk of injury. (See the *Coaches Guide to Sport Physiology* [Sharkey, 1986] for more ideas on warming up your athletes.)

Practice Previously Taught Skills. Previously taught skills, especially those needing improvement, should always receive a certain amount of practice time. Carefully selected drills that provide numerous practice opportunities are ideal. These drills should be (a) fun and safe to perform, (b) designed so that they are consistent with the practice principles presented later in this chapter, and (c) effective for learning the skill. From time to time it is a good idea to let your team help design or choose some of the drills. However, whatever you do, *don't drill so much that it becomes monotonous for your athletes.*

You should review the key learning points before having the team practice a skill and, if necessary, give a demonstration. Once the athletes have been reminded how to perform the skill and understand how to proceed with the drill, they can begin practicing. If possible, arrange the athletes in a formation that will allow them to move quickly to the actual practice from their positions during your review or demonstrations. While they are practicing, try to move from one athlete to another, giving feedback as needed.

This is an excellent time to help the athletes individualize their practice. Encourage them to practice skills needing more work. As long as they are practicing safely and not developing bad habits, let them choose their own practice methods.

Teach and Practice New Skills. The four major steps for teaching a new skill are as follows:

1. Introduce the skill.
2. Demonstrate and briefly explain the skill.
3. Have the team begin to practice the skill.
4. Provide feedback to correct errors.

These steps will be discussed in detail in chapters 3 through 9. For now, however, here are 10 practice principles to keep in mind whenever you are teaching sport skills.

1. Practice the skill in contest-like conditions as soon as athletes are able to do so.
2. Practice periods should be short and frequent when your athletes are learning a new skill.
3. Each athlete should be working throughout the practice on some aspect of the sport.

4. Practice conditions should make maximum use of available facilities and equipment.
5. The athletes should experience a reasonable amount of success at each practice.
6. Create a practice atmosphere in which the athletes are not afraid of making mistakes.
7. Let your athletes help you plan practices.
8. Frequently emphasize that practices are for improving skills.
9. Allot time for practicing skills that need improvement.
10. Make practices fun.

Practice Under Competitive Conditions. This segment of the practice should be devoted to practicing skills under simulated contest conditions, which should bring the session to a close on a high note. This does not mean, however, that your team should be left unsupervised or should practice without a purpose. On the contrary, you should also direct and control this portion of practice time in accordance with your specific performance objectives. The direction and control, however, should not be overbearing.

Cool-Down. Many coaches neglect the cool-down period, a decision that risks injury to the athletes. A few minutes spent in slowly returning the body to its resting state helps remove the waste products of exercise from the blood stream. Additional stretching is also helpful. (For more information consult the *Coaches Guide to Sport Physiology* [Sharkey, 1986].)

Coach's Comments. Use this part of the session to comment on how well the team practiced. Direct your comments to the whole team rather than to particular athletes. Tell them what still needs improvement and compliment them for their effort and for what they performed correctly. You may also wish to ask your athletes to evaluate the practice and offer their own suggestions for improvement. This is a good time to discuss briefly what you plan to do at the next practice, and, again, you may wish to request suggestions from the team. Finally, inform the team of the time and place of the next practice and mention any other important information they should know before the next practice.

Implement and Evaluate the Practice Session

Before you implement your practice plan and actually conduct the practice, meet with your assistant coaches and review the plan so that everyone knows his or her responsibilities during the practice. After conducting the practice, evaluate it as soon as possible. Indicate whether or not the performance objectives were achieved. Consider your team's suggestions and ask the assistant coaches to contribute to the evaluation. In addition, include anything else you may have observed about the practice session that you think is important to record. Also, don't forget periodically to evaluate your teaching effectiveness and that of your assistant coaches using the Teaching Evaluation Scale, which can be found in chapter 10 of *Coaching Young Athletes* (Martens et al., 1981).

POSTSEASON INSTRUCTIONAL EVALUATION

The last two steps illustrated in Figure 1.1 constitute your major coaching responsibilities that have to be performed during the postseason instructional evaluation. These steps are not included in *Coaching Young Athletes* (Martens et al., 1981), so the information presented in this section will be new.

Step 6: Evaluate Athletes' Outgoing Knowledge and Skill Level

During the last few practices you should evaluate your athletes' outgoing knowledge and skill level according to your instructional schedule and goals. This should be done for two reasons:

- It will help you select the information, behaviors, and sport skills to teach to your returning athletes next season. If you do not plan to coach next season, complete the postseason evaluation form and pass it on to the individual who will be coaching.

- Compare the postseason evaluation with your preseason evaluation. This will enable you to determine the extent to which the team progressed through your instructional schedule and achieved your instructional goals. Reviewing these evaluations side by side will not only inform you about how much your athletes have learned from the beginning to the end of the season but will also reveal what they need to practice during the off-season.

Use the Team Evaluation Form (see Figure 1.2) to conduct the postseason evaluation. This is the same format you used to assess your athletes' incoming knowledge and skill level during the preseason. In addition, you should complete a copy of the Athlete Evaluation Form (see Figure 1.3) for each athlete at the end of the season. Review the form with each athlete individually and focus on two key topics. First, discuss his or her personal learning goals and the extent to which these were achieved. Second, discuss your expectations and evaluate the extent to which they were achieved. Make certain that you indicate how much the athlete has learned over the course of the season; sometimes your athletes will not realize how much they've improved. You need to make them aware of their progress; this information can give them a strong sense of accomplishment as well as enhance their self-worth. It may also motivate them to want to learn more and to continue in your program. If an athlete expresses an interest, you can use the Athlete Evaluation Form to point out the skills he or she needs to practice in the off-season. Above all, finish the season on a *positive* note and emphasize the athlete's successes rather than his or her failures.

Using the Athlete Evaluation Form properly places emphasis on each athlete's individual progress and does not compare his or her achievements to those of others. This form can be an invaluable learning tool as long as you don't *openly* compare the learning accomplishments of one athlete with those of another. Moreover, used properly, it will enable you to emphasize what the athlete has learned or areas in which the athlete has improved, an important measure of success. All too often coaches fail to do this because too much emphasis has been placed on *winning* as the primary or even the sole measure of success.

Step 7: Evaluate Entire Instructional Program and Coaching Staff

The last step in the instructional process is evaluation of your entire program, yourself, and your assistant coaches. To accomplish this step you will need to use the information you have already assembled in Steps 4 and 6. You will also need to compose one or more evaluation forms that your athletes, assistant coaches, and parents can use to evaluate your program and the teaching effectiveness of those associated with it. An example of this type of form is shown in Figure 1.5.

Once you have put all of this evaluative information together, meet with your assistant coaches and cooperatively interpret the information. Determine the aspects of the program that should remain unchanged and the parts needing revision and then make the appropriate changes. Next, you and your assistant coaches should meet to interpret the information evaluating each of you as a teacher. Discuss each coach's strengths and weaknesses and develop a consensus on specific ways in which the weaknesses can be remedied. Once the program and the coaches have been evaluated, the program revisions have been implemented, and the recommendations for improving teaching effectiveness have been put forward, your instructional responsibilities for the season are completed. Furthermore, your instructional program for the next season should be ready to go.

SUMMARY CHECKLIST

In this chapter we have identified your major instructional responsibilities for a single season. We have provided the following check list to help you remember these responsibilities.

Instructions: Rate each item on the following scale: BA = below average, A = average; AA = above average; NA = not applicable. Circle only one per item.

Instructional Program Attributes (1-10)

1. Appropriateness of instructional goals	BA	A	AA	NA
2. Appropriateness of subject matter selected to achieve instructional goals	BA	A	AA	NA
3. Organization of subject matter for instruction over the entire season	BA	A	AA	NA
4. Pace of the instruction over the entire season	BA	A	AA	NA
5. Organization of practices	BA	A	AA	NA
6. Suitability of instructional materials for practices	BA	A	AA	NA
7. Suitability of instructional methods for practices	BA	A	AA	NA
8. Amount of individualization of instruction	BA	A	AA	NA
9. Quality of evaluation of athletes' knowledge, skill level, and learning progress	BA	A	AA	NA
10. Overall rating of instructional program for the season	BA	A	AA	NA

Coach's Teaching Attributes (11-20)

11. Knowledge of subject matter	BA	A	AA	NA
12. Interest in teaching the subject matter	BA	A	AA	NA
13. Empathy in teaching the athletes	BA	A	AA	NA
14. Preparation for practices	BA	A	AA	NA
15. Effectiveness in designing practice conditions (drills, etc.) for learning	BA	A	AA	NA
16. Clarity of explanations and demonstrations	BA	A	AA	NA
17. Effectiveness in diagnosing performance errors and using feedback to make corrections	BA	A	AA	NA
18. Influence on athletes' motivation to learn	BA	A	AA	NA
19. Attitude toward athletes	BA	A	AA	NA
20. Overall rating of coach as a teacher	BA	A	AA	NA

Open Comments

---

1. What did you like best about the program?

2. What did you like least about the program?

3. What suggestions do you have for improving this program?

Figure 1.5 Instructional evaluation form for the season.

Checklist of Instructional Responsibilities

Preseason Instructional Planning Responsibilities

Step 1: Establish instructional goals

_____ Write each goal as a general statement specifying (a) the performance in observable and measurable terms, (b) the conditions under which the performance is to occur, and (c) the standard that indicates when it is achieved.

_____ Share the goals with the assistant coaches, team, and parents.

Step 2: Select the subject matter for each goal

_____ Select subject matter from the instructional goals by asking yourself what the athletes need to learn to achieve each of the goals.

_____ Determine if the selected subject matter is appropriate and safe for the athletes on the team.

Step 3: Organize the subject matter for instruction

_____ For each goal, develop a tentative instructional schedule that outlines (a) what to teach and practice, (b) when to do it, and (c) how much time to spend on it.

Step 4: Evaluate athletes' incoming knowledge and skill level

_____ During the first few practices of the season, evaluate what each athlete knows or is able to do in comparison with what the instructional schedule expects him or her to know or be able to do.

_____ Use the evaluation results to revise the instructional schedule and to identify the subject matter that needs to be (a) reviewed and practiced by each athlete as previously learned material and (b) learned and practiced by each athlete as new material.

_____ Give each athlete his or her evaluation results and discuss them in relation to the instructional goals and the athlete's personal learning goals. Focus the discussion on the subject matter to be learned during the upcoming season.

In-Season Instructional Responsibilities

Step 5: Plan, implement, and evaluate each practice

_____ Prepare the practice plan in advance by selecting the subject matter from the instructional schedule while taking into account the athletes' progress from the previous practices, input from athletes and assistant coaches, and practice time available to prepare the athletes for the next competition.

_____ Record date of practice.

_____ Write performance objectives derived from the instructional schedule that are specific statements identifying (a) the performance in observable and measurable terms, (b) the conditions under which the performance is to occur, and (c) the standard according to which it is achieved.

_____ Prepare both practice equipment and the practice area.

_____ Allot time for warm-up and specify method(s).

_____ Allot time to practice previously taught skills and determine method(s).

_____ Allot time to teach and practice new skills and specify method(s).

_____ Allot time to practice under contest-like conditions and determine method(s).

_____ Allot time to bring the team together at the end of practice for comments.

_____ Provide the opportunity for the athletes and coaching staff to evaluate the practice.

_____ Meet with assistant coaches before the practice to review the plan.

Postseason Instructional Evaluation Responsibilities

Step 6: Evaluate athletes' outgoing knowledge and skill level

_____ During the last few practices of the season, evaluate what each athlete knows or is able to do in relation to what the instructional schedules expected him or her to know or be able to do.

_____ Compare the postseason and preseason evaluation results to determine the extent to which each athlete progressed over the course of the instructional schedule and achieved the instructional goals.

_____ Give each athlete his or her evaluation results and discuss them in relation to the preseason evaluation results to determine how much was learned during the season. Focus on the extent to which both the athlete's personal learning goals and the instructional goals were achieved.

Step 7: Evaluate entire instructional program and coaching staff

_____ Employ the evaluation results from Steps 4 and 6 to determine for next season the subject matter that needs to be (a) reviewed and practiced as previously learned material and (b) learned and practiced as new material.

_____ Have the athletes, assistant coaches, and parents evaluate the entire instructional program and teaching effectiveness of the coaches.

_____ Meet with assistant coaches, cooperatively interpret the evaluation results for the whole program and the teaching effectiveness of each coach, and cooperatively make specific recommendations for improving both.

Chapter 2
Understanding the Process of Learning Skills

The previous chapter described your instructional responsibilities for a single season and made the point that meeting your responsibilities will help your athletes learn sport skills. Chapter 2 will introduce you to the stages athletes go through as they learn. This information will help you understand the skill-learning process, will tell you what to be aware of as athletes learn skills, and will be invaluable in helping you adapt your teaching to the learning needs of your athletes. We will discuss the following topics:

- Skill learning: an invisible process
- The beginning stage of skill learning
- The intermediate stage of skill learning
- The advanced stage of skill learning

SKILL LEARNING: AN INVISIBLE PROCESS

Skill learning is an invisible process by which performance originates or is changed as a result of practice. If we teach an athlete a new skill, such as a handstand in gymnastics, the athlete is then able to execute it for the very first time, crude though it may be, and thereafter continues to improve his or her form and balance with practice, we conclude that the athlete is learning. But how did we reach this conclusion? We did not observe the learning directly because it is an internal process taking place within the athlete's central nervous system. In other words, the learning process itself is invisible to us. However, we did ob-

serve the original handstand performance and the improvement in performance made by the athlete from one practice trial to the next, and we thus inferred that learning was taking place. Furthermore, if we had observed no improvement in handstand performance, we would have concluded that no learning was taking place.

As a general rule, then, the visible evidence of performance tells us whether or not learning has occurred. However, we should make this type of inference very cautiously because it is easy to be mistaken. For instance before we infer that no learning is taking place because we see no improvement in performance, we must be certain to take account of variables that affect performance but do not affect learning. Consider, for example, the following situations:

- An athlete is learning, but his or her personal problems interfere with showing the performance improvement at a particular practice.
- An athlete is learning, but an injury of which you are unaware is preventing him or her from showing the performance improvement acquired.

Although learning is taking place in each of these examples, performance variables are preventing demonstration of learning. The more we understand such variables, the more likely we are to make correct inferences about the invisible process of learning.

Skill learning may also be thought of as a continuous process that consists of three stages—beginning, intermediate, and advanced. However, to think of these stages as distinct would be misleading because one stage blends progressively into another as learning proceeds, and no clear transitions between the stages are evident. Your role as a teacher of skills is to help your athletes progress through these learning stages as efficiently and effectively as possible. Your teaching should *cause* them to learn the skill correctly and more quickly than if they were to try to learn it by themselves. Chapters 3 through 13 will explain in more detail how you can accomplish these goals. The remainder of this chapter will focus on helping you understand the skill-learning process and the changes athletes go through at each stage as they learn.

THE BEGINNING STAGE OF SKILL LEARNING

Your athletes need to do three things in the beginning stage of learning a new skill:

- Recognize the previously learned movement patterns that can be used in learning the new skill.
- Learn the new movement patterns that are required to perform the new skill.
- Integrate and arrange the previously learned movement patterns and the new movement patterns into the sequence of movements that constitute the new skill. At this stage of learning a new skill, previously learned movement patterns are changed into new patterns. (Chapter 7, which discusses teaching for positive transfer between skills, will show you how to take advantage of transferring previously learned patterns in your teaching.)

Teaching a skill during the beginning stage usually involves three major steps: First, verbally introduce the skill; second, demonstrate and briefly explain the skill; and third, help your athletes to perform the skill well enough to begin practicing it. (Chapters 3 through 5

explain these three teaching steps in detail.) We will now consider how each of these steps influences an athlete's skill learning at this stage of the process.

Developing a Motor Program

The brief verbal introduction should provide your athletes with a positive frame of mind for learning the skill you are about to demonstrate and explain. It should hold their attention, give them information about the skill to be learned, and motivate them by furnishing a reason for learning the skill. Once the introduction is over, your athletes are ready for the demonstration and a brief explanation of the skill. The demonstration shows the athletes how the skill should be performed, and the explanation briefly describes the actions of the skill and directs the team's attention to a *few* of the most important things to watch for or think about as the skill is being demonstrated. When properly done, the introduction, demonstration, and explanation of the skill give your athletes a basic understanding of how to perform the skill. This understanding will enable them to begin to construct a *motor program*, or mental representation, that is suitable for controlling their performance of the skill.

A motor program resembles a computer program, and learning a motor program is similar to developing a computer program. Just as a computer needs instructions—the program—to perform a task, your body needs a set of instructions to guide movement. Thus a motor program may be thought of as a sequence of general instructions that an athlete's nervous and muscular systems must carry out for the successful production of the movements that make up the skill. These general instructions are written in the language of the nervous system, and each instruction is transmitted by way of that system. Ultimately, the athlete's muscular system is called upon to perform the skill.

We rarely write a computer program perfectly on the first attempt, but we learn from correcting our initial errors and eventually modify the program until it runs successfully. The same procedure is followed by athletes learning a motor program. As your athletes listen (to your introduction and explanation) and watch (your demonstration), each one is beginning to develop a set of instructions. Next, he or she attempts to perform the new skill, which gives the athlete the opportunity to try out his or her motor program for executing the skill to see if it works properly. If it does, the motor program is working efficiently. But if it doesn't, the athlete will begin to revise it based on (a) what he or she experienced while trying to perform the skill, (b) the feedback he or she received as a natural consequence of the performance, and (c) the feedback that you provided. It is worth noting here that this entire process appears to demand a great deal of your athlete's attention. They seem unable to attend to anything else while they are making their first few attempts to perform the skill.

Duration of the Beginning Stage

The beginning stage of learning may take only a few minutes, like teaching a simple skill to older athletes, or it may involve a longer period such as teaching a new, complex skill to younger athletes. You can often decrease the length of time it takes to learn a motor program by alerting your athletes to the similarity in movement patterns between a previously learned skill and the new skill you are teaching. If the old and new skills are similar then a motor program is already in place and needs only modification to accommodate the new

skills. Once you advise your athletes of the similarity, they can use parts of their previously learned motor program to construct the new one.

The beginning stage is complete when your athletes are able to perform the skill in a reasonable approximation of the way it was demonstrated. They may now begin practicing. Don't be surprised, however, to see many errors in their first few performance attempts because their motor program is largely undeveloped at this stage of learning and far from its final form.

THE INTERMEDIATE STAGE OF SKILL LEARNING

After your athletes understand how to execute the skill and can perform it in an acceptable way, they must practice it to perfect it. However, it is important to realize that practice alone is insufficient for learning a skill correctly. For practice to be effective, your athletes (a) must be motivated to learn; (b) need to attend to the relevant cue(s) and/or strategy; (c) have to receive instructional feedback both on what they are doing correctly and incorrectly and on how their errors can be corrected; and (d) must receive reinforcement, which can come from experiencing a correct performance or from the feedback offered by you, your assistant coaches, or teammates, such as when compliments are given to an athlete for performing the skill properly or for trying to perform it properly. (You will learn more about practice, feedback, and similar components of learning in chapters 6 through 9.)

Duration of the Intermediate Stage

The intermediate stage of learning requires varying amounts of time, depending on the complexity of the skill, the capabilities of the athlete, and the quality of the instruction and training. Learning simple skills may take only a few hours, whereas mastering complex skills may take years. As a general rule, this stage is complete when the athletes begin to perform the skill accurately and consistently. However, during the intermediate stage neither their form nor the outcome of their performance are as correct and regular as they could be. When your athletes are able to perform the skill automatically, they will have reached the advanced stage of learning.

Performance Improvements

At the outset of the intermediate stage of learning, your athletes have not yet established in memory, due to their limited experience with the skill, a perception for what the skill should feel like when it is performed correctly. Consequently, they cannot evaluate whether or not their movements were made properly and must rely almost entirely on your instructional feedback. As practice continues and the athletes progress through this phase of learning, they will begin to develop a perception for what the skill should feel like when they perform it as they intended. This perception occurs only with practice and probably develops in the following manner.

Your athletes' performance errors are large at the beginning of this stage of learning and they experience the feelings or sensations associated with these incorrect movements. On each practice trial your athletes attempt to reduce their previous errors by relating feedback about the outcome of their performance to their memories of previous sensations. The athletes are very dependent on instructional feedback from you to develop the correct movement pattern and thus to remember sensations associated with the correct movement pattern. Later in the intermediate phase of learning, the athletes can readily reproduce the correct or nearly correct movement pattern without your feedback. Furthermore, the athletes can then evaluate the correctness of their movement pattern by comparing the sensations arising from the movement pattern they just performed with the sensations they have in memory about what the pattern should feel like when it is performed correctly.

As your athletes practice and progress through this stage of learning, many changes will occur in them and in their performance of the skill if they are learning it correctly. You can expect the following important changes:

- Improved accuracy
- Increased consistency
- Decreased energy expenditure
- Increased speed and improved timing
- Increased anticipation/increased automation
- Decreased self-talk
- Increased self-confidence
- Improved motor programs
- Increased use of relevant motor abilities

Improved Accuracy

Your athletes' performance will increasingly resemble the correct movement pattern. For example, a gymnast's form for a handstand will become more and more like the form expected by the judges. But improvement is not limited to skills emphasizing form, such as gymnastics, diving, and figure skating. In skills whose goal is to produce an outcome, such as a pass in soccer or shot in basketball, the outcome itself will improve in accuracy.

Increased Consistency

Your athletes' form when performing the skill will become more consistent. For instance, as gymnasts, figure skaters, and divers continue to practice and progress through the intermediate stage of learning, their form not only becomes more like the correct form but is repeated more regularly. If the goal is to produce an outcome, such as a pass in soccer or a shot in basketball, it will occur both more consistently and more accurately.

Decreased Energy Expenditure

At the beginning of the intermediate stage, your athletes will exert a tremendous amount of energy and use their muscles inefficiently. As they continue to practice and progress through the intermediate stage, however, technique will improve, extraneous actions will be eliminated, and they will use less energy in performing the skill than they did as the stage began. This change will enable the athletes to achieve faster performances or participate for a longer time.

Improved efficiency in performance is easily observable in swimming. Beginning swimmers normally take far too many strokes, get too little power from each stroke, and become quickly fatigued. Because of problems with body position and stroke mechanics, the swimmer has to work hard to travel the length of the pool. Later in the intermediate stage of learning, as confidence and skill level increase, coaches might stress taking fewer strokes but making each stroke cover more distance. One way to do this would be to have swimmers count the number of strokes per length of the swimming pool and gradually try to reduce this number. In time the swimmers will be able to swim faster and for longer distances, and their movements will be much more fluid. The same principle applies in distance running, cross-country skiing, cycling, skating, and many other sports.

Increased Speed and Improved Timing

Many sport skills must be performed quickly and accurately, such as the tennis serve, the golf swing, and the penalty kick in soccer. Early in the intermediate stage of learning, your athletes have to compromise between speed and accuracy. For example, it is difficult for a beginner to increase the speed of a tennis serve or golf swing to hit the ball hard without sacrificing accuracy. But in the intermediate stage your athletes will develop the proper timing to be able to increase speed without sacrificing accuracy because they will have developed a more efficient motor program. Increased speed and proper timing can also be enhanced through improved physical conditioning. (You will learn more about how to teach skills that require both speed and accuracy in chapter 6.)

Increased Automation

Athletes seem to need to pay less conscious attention to how to execute the skill as they progress through the intermediate stage. As toddlers we have to concentrate on the technique of walking; now, of course, we walk automatically. When a skill becomes more highly developed later in the intermediate stage, it can also be performed automatically. Beginning basketball players have difficulty talking to you while they are dribbling the ball; if they try to talk, they lose control of the ball. As your athletes progress through the intermediate stage, they will be able to simultaneously dribble and talk. They are then able to perform more than one skill at a time and focus on several different performance goals. Moreover, when they are not attending solely to skill performance, athletes are able to focus on relevant cues in the environment that can influence their play. In addition, they can integrate their movements with those of other players and adapt to environmental changes. (You will learn more about attention and concentration in chapter 12.)

Increased Anticipation

As practice continues and more experience is gained, your athletes will learn to react less and to anticipate better the predictable events in their sport. They will more effectively anticipate necessary responses and when to make them. For example, beginning baseball players first learning to catch high fly balls have considerable difficulty anticipating where the ball will be and when it will be there. As a result, they frequently misjudge fly balls and have to react at the last second to try to make the catch. However, athletes in the intermediate stage learn to anticipate the flight of the ball and are better able to prepare in advance to position themselves to make the play. (You will learn more about anticipation and quick reaction in chapter 11.)

Decreased Self-Talk

Some of your athletes may never completely stop talking to themselves, even in the advanced stage of learning. However, they will tend to do so less as they progress through the intermediate stage of learning and their skill level improves. Much self-talk is actually instructive and can be useful in learning and performing skills. For example, you can quite often hear golfers using verbal labels associated with the key elements of performing the skill. Immediately before golfers swing they might say, "Low and slow," to emphasize concentrating on keeping the club head low to the ground on the backswing and making a slow, smooth backswing. You can also hear athletes talking to themselves while analyzing their own incorrect technique and searching for ways to improve it. However, not all self-talk is instructive, and some of it seems to be an emotional reaction to a poor performance. For instance, how often have you heard athletes criticizing themselves for failing to perform a skill correctly or as expected? In any case, regardless of its origin or purpose, self-talk, a natural part of the skill-learning process, appears to decrease as athletes progress through the intermediate stage.

Increased Self-Confidence

As your athletes learn, they will become more confident in their ability to perform the skill, and increased self-confidence can make them feel very good about themselves and may even improve their self-concept. In addition, with increased confidence, the athletes will be more willing to learn new and more complicated skills. Fear of failure is one of the greatest inhibitions facing athletes new to a sport. Skilled coaches try to help all their athletes experience some degree of success and overcome this fear. (You will learn more about how to help your athletes overcome fear of failure in chapter 5.) Remember, improved performance leads to increased confidence, which, in turn, can cycle back to improve performance.

Improved Motor Programs

Early in the intermediate stage of learning a new skill, the motor program needed to perform the skill correctly is far from being well developed. As a result, athletes will be uncer-

tain of many aspects of movement control, such as the precise sequence in which their muscles should contract and the force of muscle contraction. Their movements will be jerky and lack coordination. If they are to improve their performance of the skill, they must improve their motor program. Computer specialists must refine a new computer program by correcting it after each run in which errors occur, and athletes must revise and reconstruct their new motor program following performance attempts in which they make errors. As athletes continue to practice and advance through the intermediate stage, instructions transmitted by their nervous system that produce successful performance will be incorporated into their motor program, and those that produce errors will be eliminated. Eventually, near the end of the intermediate stage, athletes will have a much improved motor program because it will consist mainly of instructions that they can use to perform the skill correctly. Not only is each athlete's motor program greatly improved by then, but using it repeatedly as a result of the extensive practice that takes place during this stage actually helps store it relatively securely in memory, enabling the athlete to access it whenever he or she needs to perform the skill again.

Increased Use of Relevant Motor Abilities

Motor abilities, such as speed, strength, and flexibility, are the traits or capacities of an athlete that are important to the development and performance of many different sports skills. A skill like the tennis serve, for instance, is a specific response that is learned through practice and depends on the presence of underlying motor abilities such as eye-hand coordination, balance, and power. Although each athlete's basic motor abilities are partly the result of inheritance, environmental factors play an important role in their development.

As learning progresses through the intermediate stage, we can expect changes to occur in the motor abilities each athlete uses to perform a sport skill. Specifically, we expect decreased use of nonrelevant or only slightly relevant abilities for performing the skill successfully and increased use of abilities that are relevant. For example, when athletes are first learning how to dribble a basketball, they rely very heavily on their visual ability; they look directly at the ball and their hand while they are dribbling. At a later stage in their learning, they don't appear to need their visual ability as much, if at all. They dribble the basketball quite effectively without looking directly at the ball and their hand. In fact, they could, if they had to, successfully dribble the ball with their eyes closed and not use visual information at all.

This tendency to call upon distinct and different abilities as learning progresses suggests two observations. First, athletes who early in their learning use abilities that contribute to their performance will perform the skill at a relatively high level of proficiency at the *outset* of the intermediate stage. Second, athletes who use abilities that contribute to performance later in learning will perform the skill at a relatively high level near the *end* of the intermediate stage. It is therefore unwise for coaches to assume that athletes who are able to perform a skill best when they begin to learn will be the same ones who will perform it best later in learning.

THE ADVANCED STAGE OF SKILL LEARNING

Your main responsibility during this stage of learning is to motivate your athletes to improve their skill performance so that it approaches the standard of excellence required in actual competitive situations. Your athletes' motivation depends in large part on the practice conditions you design and the feedback you provide. Once a consistently high level of skill performance is achieved, it must be maintained not only throughout a single season but also from season to season. Your athletes' motivation is the key to this achievement, and your instructional and training procedures and the effectiveness of your communication with your athletes are the keys to their motivation.

Characteristics of Athletes in the Advanced Stage

During the advanced stage your athletes' self-confidence is high, and they have a

thorough understanding of the skill. The motor program for generating the correct movements for the skill is highly developed and firmly established in memory. As a result, performance is not only consistently proficient but quite automatic as well—they seem to require very little conscious thought or attention in executing the skill. Your athletes apparently no longer need to analyze or talk to themselves about how to execute the skill during performance. In fact, performance will deteriorate if they do. Free from continually focusing on executing the skill, your athletes can now concentrate on other aspects of the game or sport. Not only is their motor program highly developed, but your athletes' perception of what the skill should feel like when it is performed as they intended to perform it is also at its peak. Consequently, athletes are now able to evaluate whether or not their movements were executed as they should have been executed.

Duration of the Advanced Stage

Despite the fact that skill performance may be approaching some arbitrary standard of perfection, you should not assume at this stage that learning is over and that performance cannot be improved. Although the level of competence an athlete may attain in a skill has certain limits, performance usually advances to this point so gradually that it is rarely possible to claim that limits have actually been achieved.

Among the factors preventing athletes from reaching their highest achievement, one is the tendency to lose motivation to strive for improvement as they approach their limit. This may occur because they think they are already extremely proficient—because they are successful and relatively unchallenged, they do not see the need to strive for greater improvement. Motivation can also be lost because practice seems to yield little or no improvement in performance. Part of this problem is that diagnosing errors to determine changes necessary for performance improvement becomes increasingly difficult for both the athlete and the coach as performance of the skill approaches perfection. The other part of the problem is that skill refinements in the advanced stage of learning tend to be difficult to make and thus come about very slowly.

This in itself can be quite discouraging to some athletes. You can help your athletes by alerting them to the probability that improvement will come slowly.

Another factor that can prevent athletes from reaching their limits has to do with the performance standards athletes set for themselves. Athletes tend to establish their own standards of perfection or excellence, and some will set them below what they are actually capable of accomplishing. Furthermore, they can become satisfied with achieving their self-established standard and refuse to push themselves further. (The *Coaches Guide to Sport Psychology* [Martens, 1987] contains excellent guidelines for setting goals.)

SUMMARY

In this chapter we introduced you to the learning process and the stages athletes go through as they learn sport skills. Keep the following points in mind as you work with your athletes:

1. Because the process of learning cannot be seen directly, you determine whether or not skill learning has occurred by observing changes in skill performance.
2. Skill learning is a continuous process consisting of three stages: beginning, intermediate, and advanced.

3. Learning a new skill involves combining previously learned movement patterns with new movement patterns.
4. Learning a skill generates a motor program, which is the neuromuscular pattern of instructions needed for controlling the performance of the skill.
5. Learning a motor program appropriate for controlling the performance of a skill is analogous to developing a computer program appropriate for controlling the performance of a computer task.
6. The main concern of teaching during the beginning stage of learning is to communicate in general terms how to perform the new skill such that the appropriate motor program may begin to develop.
7. The major concern of teaching during the intermediate stage of learning is to structure practice conditions and provide feedback that optimizes skill acquisition and motor program development.
8. As athletes proceed through the intermediate stage of learning, they develop a perception for what the skill should feel like when they perform it as they intended to.
9. Athletes experience many changes as they continue through the intermediate stage of learning a skill, such as (a) improved accuracy, consistency, efficiency, speed, and timing of skill performance; (b) increased self-confidence, anticipation, and automation in performing the skill; (c) decreased self-talk; (d) improvement of the motor program controlling the performance of the skill; and (e) increased use of abilities needed to perform the skill successfully.
10. You cannot be certain that athletes who are able to perform a skill best at the outset of the intermediate stage of learning will be able to perform it best when they reach the advanced stage of learning.
11. The main concern of teaching during the advanced stage of learning is designing practice conditions and providing feedback to motivate athletes to continue striving to perfect their skills and maintain the high level of performance they have achieved.

12. In the advanced stage of learning (a) motor programs for skills are well developed and firmly established in memory; (b) self-confidence is high, and learned skills are performed proficiently, consistently, and automatically; and (c) perception for what the learned skills should feel like when properly performed is highly developed and can be used to evaluate skill performance.

13. Reaching the advanced stage of learning does not mean that skill learning is complete. Rather, it means that the limits of competence are being approached and that learning must continue if these limits are ever to be reached.

PART II
Presenting New Skills

Based on part 1 you should know your instructional goals, what you plan to teach, how and when you plan to teach it, and how you can determine if your goals are accomplished. Now it is time to consider presenting skills effectively when teaching them to your athletes. Part 2 will tell you how to present skills with such clarity and in such a way that your athletes will know exactly what you want them to learn and why you want them to learn it. In chapter 3 you will learn how to introduce and explain skills to your athletes, and in chapter 4 you will learn how to demonstrate these skills. In addition, you will find out how to evaluate your own effectiveness at introducing, explaining, and demonstrating skills.

In chapter 5 we will suggest procedures you can use to help those athletes who are having difficulty performing a skill. In addition to repeating the explanation and demonstration, the use of part teaching methods as well as various guidance techniques and ways to minimize fear of injury and fear of failure are discussed.

Now it is time for you to discover how you can more effectively present new skills to your athletes. However, knowing how to present new skills is no guarantee that you will be able to do it successfully. After reading part 2, practice your presentation techniques so you can improve your own skill.

Chapter 3
Introducing and Explaining Skills

Have you seen any coaches who spend almost no time introducing and explaining new skills? Have you seen others who talk so much that they bore their athletes and lose valuable practice time? Do you know coaches who ramble on aimlessly, communicating practically nothing to their athletes about performing the skill or correcting their errors? Do other coaches you know deliver such a detailed, elaborate message that their athletes become confused? Are you acquainted with coaches who emphasize the introduction and explanation much more than the demonstration when teaching beginners the general idea of how to perform a skill?

These coaches are obviously not introducing and explaining skills effectively. Avoiding their mistakes requires that you take the time to learn how to introduce and explain skills properly—both are essential for effective coaching. Whether you are teaching a new skill to your athletes or correcting a well-learned skill, you'll want to use an introduction and explanation, in conjunction with a demonstration, to give your athletes a general idea of how you want the skill to be performed. (Chapter 4 is devoted to demonstrating skills effectively.)

The information in this chapter will help you learn how to introduce and explain skills effectively.

The following concepts are explored:

* Organizing your athletes for an introduction
* Delivering your introduction
* Preparing your explanation
* Delivering your explanation
* Evaluating your introduction and explanation

ORGANIZING YOUR ATHLETES FOR AN INTRODUCTION

An introduction should tell your athletes what they will be learning and why it is important; in addition, it usually prepares them for the explanation and demonstration that follow. As a result, if you want your athletes to obtain the greatest benefit from your introduction, you must make sure that you (a) get their attention and (b) organize the group so that all can see and hear.

Get Your Athletes' Attention

You will find that some athletes are very easily distracted. Young athletes, for example, may possess only rudimentary concentration skills. If you have ever coached young athletes, you know that their attention span is very short, especially if you have been unable to capture their interest initially. Teaching under this constraint is not particularly difficult if each athlete pays attention at the same time, but, as a rule, they do not. In fact, learning how to keep the attention of young athletes will always be one of your toughest coaching challenges. (You will learn more about attention in chapter 12.)

Successfully introducing a skill requires that you develop a strategy for capturing their attention initially and keeping them interested while you talk. Some coaches use interesting stories or jokes to grab their athletes' attention. Others just begin their introduction enthusiastically. When a coach is obviously enthusiastic about teaching a sport skill the enthusiasm is contagious, making athletes *want* to listen. The method you choose will depend on your personality.

Some coaches call their athletes into a circle and wait for silence, regardless of how long it takes. Unfortunately, this technique has the disadvantage of punishing those atheletes who are eager to begin. The interested athletes may eventually realize that their time is being wasted, and they may ask their noisy classmates to keep quiet. But making athletes sit and wait opens the door for others to begin conversations. As your coaching experience grows, you will develop and refine your technique to reflect your own personality and take account of the various personalities of your athletes.

Here are some general organizational principles that many coaches have found effective:

- Develop a regular routine for starting practice; go to your usual place at the beginning of practice and blow a whistle or give some other obvious sign to announce that you want everybody's attention.
- Once you are in position facing your athletes, make eye contact with each one and tell the group what you have planned for them.
- Speak firmly, politely, and slightly louder than normal conversational level. When a few of your athletes are inattentive, look directly at them, move closer to them if necessary, and firmly but politely address them by name and ask for their attention.

- If this does not work, you can use some form of punishment, such as asking the athlete to leave the group and stand in a corner of the gym or field until you have finished your introduction.

Arrange Your Athletes So That All Can See and Hear

The way you arrange your athletes when speaking to them will influence how well they pay attention to you. If athletes mill around or crowd together, getting and maintaining their attention is often very difficult. Figure 3.1 illustrates two examples of team formations useful for introductions and explanations. Of course, other formations are effective. (Be sure to consider the factors concerning formations that chapter 4 discusses.)

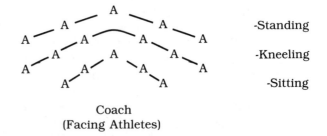

Figure 3.1 Team formations for introductions and explanations.

In general, make certain that the background your athletes see behind you is free from visual distractions. When you are sharing a gym or playing field with another group, position yourself so that your athletes will not see the other group. If you are coaching out of doors, do not make your athletes face the sun. Finally, select an area having minimum background noise so that they can hear you.

DELIVERING YOUR INTRODUCTION

Once your athletes are properly arranged, how do you deliver an effective introduction? Make it *brief, simple, and direct.* It should mentally prepare your athletes for learning the skill that is about to be explained and demonstrated. It should tell the athletes what they are going to learn and why they need to learn it. Avoid introductions that are too detailed, elaborate, or abstract—they take so long to present that they delay the demonstration, which is usually the most effective way to show your athletes what you want them to do. Furthermore, a wordy introduction has limited meaning for your athletes until they have seen how the skill or correction should be executed and have had some experience performing it.

A basketball coach might effectively introduce a left-handed lay-up as follows:

Now that you've learned how to shoot a lay-up with your right hand, I am going to teach you how to make the same shot with your left hand. Being able to use either hand is important because it will allow you to shoot from either side of the basket. This ability will make it more difficult for your opponent to guard you, and you'll score more.

Notice that although this introduction is brief, it explains which skill the athletes will be learning and why it will be valuable to them. The way you introduce a skill will influence how well your athletes will understand and learn it. Pay particular attention to the language you use when teaching athletes and keep it appropriate to the age level you are coaching. For example, young athletes may not understand expressions like *get into pairs* or *get into groups of three* unless you provide additional explanation or even physical assistance, although older athletes should have no difficulty understanding you.

You should remember this important fact: Because words alone have little meaning to athletes who are learning a skill for the first time, your verbal introduction will have limited value at the outset of learning in communicating the general idea of how to perform a skill. Beginners will not yet have linked the words to the movement required to perform the skill. Before your athletes can understand and benefit from your presentation, they must construct a movement vocabulary by practicing and experiencing the skill. At that stage of learning when their movement vocabulary is formed, your comments about how they moved or should have moved will become more meaningful. Finally, use the introduction to increase your athletes' motivation to learn the skill by not only explaining its value but also pointing out well-known or successful athletes who use the technique.

PREPARING YOUR EXPLANATION

Like an effective introduction, an effective explanation of a skill requires careful planning before it is delivered. Be certain that you (a) select the best words, (b) relate what you are teaching to previous learning, and (c) consider the use of verbal pretraining.

Select the Best Words

Some words more effectively explain how to perform skills than others. Quite often, the words you choose will directly and literally communicate what you want your athletes to do. For example, when describing a wrestling stance you might say, "Stand with your feet shoulder-width apart, knees slightly bent, head up, and back straight." Sometimes, however, a direct, literal description becomes too awkward and detailed, and then a figurative explanation can be much more effective. For example, when teaching your basketball players how to follow through on a one-handed jump shot, you could literally describe the action of the arm, hand, wrist, and fingers in this way: "After you release the ball, be certain that your arm is extended at the elbow, your wrist is bent (flexed), and your fingers are relatively straight (extended) just above and toward the rim of the basket." However, you will get better results if you use a figurative description: "After you release the ball, dunk your fingers over the rim and into the basket."

In some instances a combination of literal

and figurative descriptions is useful. When teaching athletes to use less grip pressure on equipment like baseball or softball bats, tennis racquets, or golf clubs, you might say, ''Grip the golf club with less pressure when you swing.'' Although this is helpful advice, it does not give your athletes a specific idea of how much pressure to apply when gripping the club. They will understand you better if you add a figurative phrase:

> Imagine that the club you are going to swing is a tube of toothpaste without a cap. If your grip is too tight, the toothpaste will squirt out, and if you don't grip it tightly enough, the whole tube will fly out of your hands when you swing. Grip it tightly enough to hold it in your hands when you swing but not so tightly that the toothpaste will squirt out.

Remember, literal descriptions work best for some skills, figurative descriptions work best for others, and at times a combination of the two is your most effective choice. When selecting the type of explanation to use, the most important consideration is the effect produced, that is, whether it results in the desired action.

Relate What You Are Teaching to Previous Learning

Athletes skilled in one sport are often surprised at the ease with which they can learn some new skills and the difficulty of learning others. Similarities of movements and the use of common principles can make it easier to learn certain new skills. For example, a tennis player learning how to play badminton might find learning racquet control and court movement quite easy because of the similarities between the games. But learning to make effective smash and lob shots might prove more difficult because tennis does not include the necessary pattern of wrist action. In fact, tennis players try to avoid snapping the wrist too much.

Teaching any skill to your athletes will have better results if your explanation relates the new skill to others they have already learned. This is the principle of *transfer of learning*, the effect learning one skill has on the subsequent learning of other skills. Athletes who understand that a previously learned skill or a part of that skill can be transferred to the new skill can usually learn the new skill more quickly than if they lacked that understanding. For example, when someone is trying to learn the tennis serve for the first time and is having difficulty moving the racquet through the proper sequence of movements, you can assist him or her by explaining and demonstrating how these movements are similar to and different from the previously learned skill of throwing a ball overhand.

The transfer-of-learning principle also applies to teaching new plays and strategies to your team. For instance, at a basketball practice a team is learning the give-and-go play for the first time. In this play, one player passes the ball to a teammate, runs toward the basket, and looks for a return pass from the teammate. It can be very helpful to explain and demonstrate to the team that this play is similar to the give-and-go play they already learned in soccer.

Explaining relationships to enhance transfer of learning is not limited to movement skills and team plays. It can also be used to transfer previously learned mechanical principles, thus informing athletes why a certain technique or form is successful. For example, the principle of stability states that, other things being equal, the lower the center of gravity, the greater the stability of the body. Thus we see a gymnast on a balance beam rapidly squat when losing balance, and a wrestler quickly bend the knees when being forced off balance by the opponent. Athletes who understand this principle can be taught how to apply it to help them perform various skills. However, this approach is neither the quickest nor most efficient way to get athletes to perform a skill well enough to begin practicing it; the quickest way is to demonstrate and explain simply and directly the technique you want them to initiate—simply show and tell them how to perform the skill.

What, then, is the value of including one or more mechanical principles as part of the explanation at the outset of learning a skill? It is to increase the rate of learning *other* new skills that make use of the newly explained principle. Understanding a principle inherent in one skill and being able to apply it to performing that skill should transfer to the learning of other skills making use of the same principle. Understanding the principle of stability, for instance, as it applies to wrestling and utilizing it during matches should be transferable to learning defensive line play in football. If a wrestler has learned to lower his center of gravity for increased stability against an opponent, that principle should be available for teaching the athlete how to increase his stability or balance against an offensive lineman who is trying to block him.

Although this reasoning appears to be valid, research has not yet shown conclusively that one or more mechanical principles included as part of the introduction at the outset of learning a skill are readily transferable. In the realm of scientific research into transferring *principles*, we think principles could be demonstrated if the principles were introduced later in learning, after athletes have had a considerable amount of experience practicing the skill. They may need to have physically experienced the execution of the skill before they can understand the relationship between the execution and the mechanical principle or principles underlying the execution. In fact, an experience-based understanding of how and why a skill is executed in a particular way might contribute not only to a faster rate of learning other new skills using the sample principles but might also help athletes in later stages of learning analyze their own performances and make corrections without the coach's assistance.

In summary, in all of these examples you are helping your athletes relate already-learned skills and principles to new skills that they are about to learn. If they understand these relationships, they increase their chances of transferring identical or similar parts of their previous learning to learning the new skill, play, or principle. The athletes will also know which parts of the skill must be learned for the first time. If you can communicate these relationships effectively, the athletes will efficiently integrate the previously learned parts and the newly learned parts into the series of parts that make up the skill, strategy, principle, or play that you want them to learn. Remember, if you want to ensure that transfer of learning is going to occur, you must teach it directly and not leave it to chance. (Chapter 7 provides more detailed information on how you can teach for positive transfer.)

Verbal Pretraining

Have you ever tried to learn a skill, such as ballroom dancing, that requires a complex sequence of movements? If so, you may have experienced frustrations similar to those faced by your athletes. One way to improve your teaching of complex movement skills is using *verbal pretraining.* You supply simple word labels to help remind your athletes of what to do next while executing a complex skill. Once mastered, these labels identify the steps in the sequence simply and directly, and they make preparing for the practice and learning the skills much easier.

Verbal pretraining should be a part of your explanation. Although not effective for all athletes or for learning all skills, this technique is very useful when athletes have to learn a sequence of actions or procedures that is initially difficult to remember. Examples of such skills include (a) a football quarterback executing a complex running play or a play-action pass, (b) a track athlete performing the triple jump or discus throw, and (c) a gymnast doing a backward roll with a back extension from a standing position.

Let's consider one example in detail. Assume you are coaching baseball and are preparing to introduce your athletes to the footwork required by a second baseman in making a double play when receiving a throw from the shortstop. Figure 3.2 depicts the sequence of skills needed to execute this play.

Figure 3.2 The footwork required by a second baseman in making a double play when receiving a throw from a shortstop.

How might you best teach this movement sequence to your athletes? One way would be to use verbal pretraining in the following manner. Tell them that the word *left* means to step on the base with the left foot and catch the ball, *right* means to take a step with the right foot toward the shortstop after the catch, and *left* means to step with the left foot toward first base and throw the ball to that base. Demonstrate the sequence as you explain the labels. You may want to repeat the demonstration and a shortened explanation several times and have the athletes say the words *left-right-left* as each step in the sequence is performed. Now you can set up the drill to practice the double play with the expectation that rehearsing left-right-left will help your athletes remember the sequence of steps in making the double play.

The verbal pretraining principle can be used in many sports. Be sure to use simple, direct labels that describe the movement or position you want your athletes to learn.

DELIVERING YOUR EXPLANATION

After introducing the skill, you will explain how it is performed and demonstrate it to your team. Like the introduction, your explanation should be appropriate to the age level of the athletes you are coaching and it should consist of language your athletes can understand. Remember to keep your explanation *brief*, *simple*, and *direct*. Excessively detailed, elaborate, or abstract explanations provide more information than athletes can digest at the onset of learning and have little or no value in communicating the basic idea of how to perform the skill. At later stages of learning, however, when your athletes can relate details or abstractions to the movements that make

up the skill, explanations encompassing these elements will become more meaningful to them.

The introductory explanation should complement your demonstration by giving the athletes a general idea of how to perform the skill—it should give them the big picture in as few words as possible. In addition, it should inform your athletes how you will conduct the demonstration and direct their attention to a few of the demonstration's most relevant cues.

Explain How the Demonstration Will Proceed

You should prepare your athletes for the demonstration of a new skill by calling for their attention and focusing it on what is about to take place. You can, for example, say the following: "Now that you know the name of the skill and why you need to learn it, let's see how to perform it. May I please have everyone look at me while I demonstrate the skill."

Next, tell your athletes how the demonstration will proceed so that they know what to expect. Also say how many times and under what conditions you will demonstrate the skill. For example:

> First I'm going to show you how the skill is performed and what it looks like in actual contest-like conditions. I'll perform it several times, changing my position each time so that everyone can see how it is done and what it looks like from different viewing angles. When I'm finished, I think you'll have enough information to be able to perform the skill.

Identify a Few of the Most Relevant Cues

In addition to explaining how the demonstration will proceed, you need to direct your athletes to focus their attention on a few of the most relevant cues included during your demonstration. These cues are sometimes more easily described than demonstrated. For instance, it is easier to tell an athlete to "put your weight over the balls of your feet" or "keep your eyes on the ball" or "grip the bat with less pressure" than it is to demonstrate these cues. However, most of the relevant cues can usually be communicated by demonstrating them. Regardless of how they are identified, remember the necessity of identifying relevant cues before the demonstration because athletes learning a skill for the first time will not recognize and focus on relevant cues as they view the skill unless you identify them beforehand. Therefore, remember to include in the demonstration of a skill brief descriptions or explanations of the most important cues.

Subdivide the Skill: Preparation, Action, and Completion

Many sport skills are more easily explained if you divide the skills into their major parts, which facilitates pointing out the relevant cues. One way to do this is to identify a skill's three components as

- preparation
- action, and
- completion

For example, the tennis forehand drive can be divided into

- the grip and stance (preparation)
- the backswing and forward swing (action) and
- the follow-through and body position at the end of the swing (completion)

Regardless of how you choose to subdivide the skill, however, always make sure that your explanation includes at least one relevant cue for each component of the skill.

This approach is used by Kerri to demonstrate the instep kick in soccer (see Figure 3.3). Instead of merely telling her players to kick the ball, she broke the skill into three different parts, and pointed out a few of the most relevant cues during a slow-motion demonstration. Thus the players learn

- how to run up to the ball and where to position the supporting leg (*preparation*)

- how to contact the ball (*action*), and
- how to follow through (*completion*).

(Chapter 7 presents additional information about dividing skills into component parts.)

Major Parts of the Skill	Demonstration and Explanation

Preparation ⟶

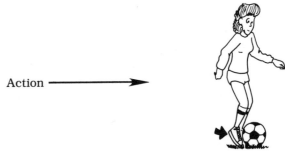

"Run up to the ball and plant your left foot next to it."

Action ⟶

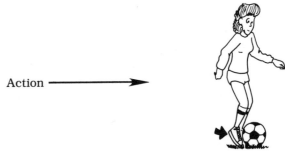

"As you strike through the ball with the center of the instep of your right foot, point your toes down, keeping the ankle rigid, and push off with your left foot."

Completion ⟶

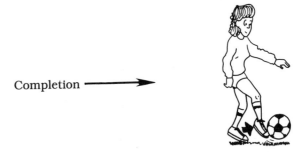

"Be certain to follow through the center of the ball toward the place you want the ball to go."

Figure 3.3 Coach Kerri explaining a few relevant cues while demonstrating the three parts of the instep kick in soccer.

EVALUATING YOUR INTRODUCTION AND EXPLANATION

Effective coaching requires something more than simply giving an introduction and explanation: You must evaluate your presentation to identify and reinforce your strengths as well as to correct your shortcomings. Have yourself videotaped, or at least audiotaped, while you are introducing and explaining a new skill. Review the presentation and determine your score on the evaluation form below. If taping equipment is unavailable have one of the assistant coaches observe your presentation and evaluate your introduction and explanation using the evaluation form.

Evaluation Form

In the column at the left, indicate the appropriate number of each item: 1 = *no* and 2 = *yes*.

1. _____ Has a regular routine for starting practice.
2. _____ Skill is introduced after the athletes have been comfortably arranged and can see and hear.
3. _____ Background viewed by the athletes is free from visual distractions (e.g., looking into the sun).
4. _____ Surrounding noise does not interfere with the athletes' ability to hear what is being said.
5. _____ Introduction begins only after the athletes have given their undivided attention.
6. _____ Controls temper and displays poise when dealing with inattentive athletes.
7. _____ Avoids annoying mannerisms, sarcasm, and abusive language.
8. _____ Uses correct grammer in presentations.
9. _____ Gives enthusiastic presentation, both verbally and nonverbally.
10. _____ Speaks clearly and loudly enough so that all can hear.
11. _____ Speaks at a speed that is appropriate for the athletes to listen and understand.
12. _____ Uses simple, direct language that is appropriate for the age level of the athletes.
13. _____ Faces team when speaking to them.
14. _____ Makes good eye contact.
15. _____ Identifies by name the skill to be demonstrated and explained.
16. _____ Specifies the goal of the skill or play if it is not obvious.
17. _____ Motivates athletes to learn the skill by giving them a reason for learning it.
18. _____ Motivates the athletes to learn the skill by identifying one or more well-known athletes who perform the skill as it is being taught.
19. _____ Introduction and explanation are brief, simple, and direct rather than long, detailed, and abstract.
20. _____ Explanation complements the demonstration and gives the athletes a general idea of how to perform the skill.
21. _____ Explains how the demonstration will proceed.
22. _____ Identifies a few of the most relevant cues.
23. _____ Uses the most effective words to explain how to perform the skill.
24. _____ Explains how the new material relates to previously learned material.
25. _____ Uses verbal pretraining, if appropriate.

Add up your 25 ratings and write the total score here _____. Compare your score with the results listed below to determine how effectively you delivered your introduction and explanation.

46–50 = superior
41–45 = above average
35–40 = average
30–34 = below average
25–29 = inferior

SUMMARY

The way you introduce and explain how to perform a skill sets the stage for how successfully your athletes will learn that skill. The following are key points for effectively introducing and explaining skills:

1. Carefully plan your introduction and explanation well before the time of delivery.
2. When organizing your athletes for the introduction be certain they (a) attend to what you say and (b) are able to see and hear you.
3. Your introduction tells your athletes what they will be learning and why it is important: It should set up the explanation and demonstration that follow.
4. When preparing your explanation, you must select effective language, relate what you are teaching to previous learning, and use verbal labels or cues to help athletes learn difficult movement sequences.
5. Your explanation should complement your demonstration by giving the athletes a general idea of how to perform the skill.
6. Your introduction and explanation should be appropriate to the age level of your athletes.
7. Your introduction and explanation should be brief, simple and direct.
8. Your explanation should specify how the demonstration will proceed and identify a few of the most relevant cues.
9. Periodically evaluate how effectively you introduce and explain skills and use the results to improve your presentations.

Chapter 4
Demonstrating Skills

Do you remember the last time you tried to learn a sport skill? What information did you need most to get an idea of what you wanted to do? It was almost certainly a demonstration or visual representation of how the skill should be performed. Whether it comes from a coach, friend, book, videotape, or television, a demonstration of the skill is extremely important at the outset of learning.

Although a clear, brief explanation lets your athletes know exactly what you want them to do, establishing the concept of a skill with a verbal explanation alone is often difficult, especially when the skill is complicated or your athletes are young or inexperienced. The best way to help your athletes understand the skill is to supplement the introduction and explanation with demonstrations designed to illustrate the specific points of technique you are explaining. The adage, A picture is worth a thousand words, is especially relevant in teaching and learning sport skills.

Whenever possible, provide a demonstration because it helps your athletes learn skills by acting as a *model* they can copy. This helps develop their understanding of a skill more firmly because they can refer to both a verbal reference, from the explanation, and a visual reference, from the demonstration.

Demonstrations are useful as a model for learning new skills and to help improve skills that have already been acquired. They are also effective for teaching team plays and strategies. To use demonstrations successfully, you must fully understand how they affect your athletes' learning. This knowledge will enable you to troubleshoot your teaching methods if your athletes are not learning from your demonstrations.

If you are to provide your athletes with effective demonstrations, you must be aware of

- how demonstrations work,
- when to use demonstrations,
- how to arrange your athletes to watch demonstrations,
- who should demonstrate,
- using film or video demonstrations and sound as a model,
- other factors to consider before giving a demonstration, and
- how to evaluate your demonstration.

HOW DEMONSTRATIONS WORK

Although demonstrations are typically coupled with explanations to present new skills and cue performance changes, how do

they work? How do athletes take the information provided by the model and use it to learn the skill? Learning from demonstrations involves four steps: attention, retention, reproduction, and motivation. Your athletes must pay attention to you and to the demonstration, remember the key points, attempt to reproduce the demonstrated movement, and be motivated to refine their initial attempts. Let's see how coaches can use these factors.

Attention

If they are not paying attention athletes cannot gain insight into how to perform a skill, whether from a demonstration or an explanation. You must first get your athletes' attention by effectively introducing the skill they are about to learn. You must also direct their attention to the key learning points of each phase of the movement, as discussed in chapter 3. Unless your athletes are paying attention to the key points, your demonstrations will be ineffective. We will discuss attention in more detail in chapter 12.

Retention

Has one of your athletes been unable to reproduce the movements of a skill even after you've demonstrated them numerous times? This situation may result if the athlete is unable to remember the key points of the movement. You will help your athletes remember more efficiently if you carefully select the cues you use to present the skills. In addition, repeat the *same* cues with each successive demonstration until they have become natural to the athletes. Another successful technique is to ask the athletes to give you cues on how to perform a skill after you've made several demonstrations. If your athletes can do this, they can remember the key points to guide their own performances. (You will find in-depth discussion of memory in chapter 11.)

Attention to and retention of the demonstration are essential for learning sport skills. It is through these first two steps that your athletes acquire a basic understanding of what you want them to do.

Reproduction

Assuming your explanation and demonstration have provided your athletes with an understanding of what you want them to do, they may still have difficulty reproducing the desired performance. What would happen, for example, if you demonstrated a driving lay-up to beginning basketball players on their first day of practice and asked them to perform the skill? Of course, many of the athletes would be unable to perform the skill correctly. Why? Athletes at this stage of learning have not yet developed the *prerequisite skills*: They must be able to dribble under control before they can dribble and shoot. If an athlete lacks prerequisite skills, he or she will be unable to reproduce the desired performance.

Help your athletes enjoy a positive outcome at this stage. Follow a logical progression of skills to enable them to perform successfully from the very beginning. Make sure that they grasp the basics and understand the principles involved. A wrestling coach, for example, should not teach advanced takedowns or throws until a wrestler has mastered the back bridge because successfully performing the back bridge is the key to weight transfer in the more advanced skills.

Arranging an appropriate progression of skills is, however, only one step toward achieving reproduction of the demonstrated performance. The key is being able to help your athletes progress from having a conceptual idea of the skill being learned to developing a motor program that can reproduce performance consistently. Strive to give your athletes a clear understanding of the skill through your demonstration and provide them with consistent, constructive feedback that will help them formulate and refine their motor program.

Motivation

The final component of the process of how demonstrations work is motivation. From time to time coaches encounter athletes who understand the demonstration, possess all the necessary skills, can repeat the key points involved in the skill, and are nevertheless unable to perform the skill correctly. What's wrong? What difficulty are these athletes experiencing? The answer is very likely to be lack of motivation to learn the new skill.

Consider the example of Cindy, a highly talented basketball player. Because she is taller than most other junior varsity ball players, Cindy has a good deal of success playing post. She pivots only off her right foot, and few defenders are able to stop her drive to the basket. Her coach, Laura, wants Cindy to learn to pivot off either foot but Cindy resists.

How can Laura motivate Cindy to add this new skill to her repertoire? She can begin by telling Cindy that she has a temporary advantage over her opponents that may disappear as they grow in height and physical ability. If she makes no attempt to improve her skills, she may well be left behind. Laura could also direct Cindy's attention to the ability of high school post players to pivot in either direction. These types of information may motivate Cindy to improve her skill level.

The Demonstration Process

Let's review the entire process. You need to get the attention of your athletes and direct it to key movements in the skill (attention). Repeat important cues so that your athletes will understand the movement you are asking them to perform and remember the key points (retention). Next, organize the demonstrations progressively to help the athletes develop their motor program sufficiently to be able to perform the skill consistently (reproduction). Finally, motivate your athletes to want to learn the new skill and/or to want to improve their current skills (motivation). The motivation component is critical in determining whether or not athletes will benefit from the demonstration process.

WHEN TO USE DEMONSTRATIONS

There are at least three different times to use demonstrations when teaching a skill: (a) before your athletes perform the skill, (b) distributed throughout a drill period, and (c) as a conclusion to the drill.

Demonstrations Before Practicing

When teaching a new skill or when teaching young athletes, who seem quickly to forget much of what they learned in the previous practice, it's advisable to precede any attempts at practicing the skill with at least one demonstration to give athletes a model to guide their performance. You will generally find that several repetitions of the demonstration are helpful. In fact, a demonstration keying each phase of the movement may be an excellent way to help athletes label and remember the parts of the skill and the accompanying movements. You may also wish to demonstrate skills from a variety of angles to give your athletes a comprehensive picture of what you want them to do.

Depending on the skill, you may need to bring the athletes together and give a formal introduction and explanation. However, with a little forethought, you can often structure your practices to lead smoothly from a review of previously taught skills to an introduction, explanation, and demonstration of new skills. Sometimes the same drills can be used for both review and demonstration, thus reducing the amount of new material. For example, if you have already taught your athletes the chest pass while they are standing in a circle formation, it is easy to use the same formation when teaching the bounce pass because the athletes are already familiar with the circle passing drill. Using the drill your athletes are already familiar with avoids intensifying their difficulties in learning this new passing technique.

Demonstrations Distributed Throughout a Drill Period

As all new coaches quickly discover, it is essential to stop practicing new skills periodically to repeat demonstrations. How you use these demonstrations depends on the age and ability of your athletes. With young athletes it is often most effective if midpractice demonstrations are the same as the first demonstration; the second demonstration reinforces the first. Young athletes do not usually have the ability to integrate what they learned from the first demonstration with any new information, and they can easily become confused. Thus, for example, when teaching 7-year-olds how to pass a soccer ball, demonstrate one technique and after a few minutes of practice demonstrate the same technique again. When coaching older athletes, on the other hand, you might be able to demonstrate a refinement of the pass in midpractice because the athletes will be sufficiently skilled to integrate the two demonstrations.

Moreover, interspersing demonstrations throughout the practice phase can be used to focus on aspects of the skill that are not being performed correctly. For instance, while observing practice, you notice that several players are watching their opponents instead of the ball. You must organize a demonstration that focuses on eliminating this specific error. Even skilled athletes need specific comments and demonstrations directed toward eliminating their weaknesses.

Demonstrations as a Conclusion

After your athletes have finished practicing a particular skill, a final demonstration is often a good idea. This demonstration will serve to reinforce your athletes' image of what the properly performed skill looks like. Many athletes think about their skills, or mentally practice them, between practice sessions. A final demonstration will help ensure that your athletes are mentally rehearsing the skill correctly. (Chapter 10 includes additional information about mental practice.)

HOW TO ARRANGE YOUR ATHLETES TO WATCH DEMONSTRATIONS

Most of the time you will find it valuable to demonstrate skills by utilizing the same general formation in which you introduce and explain skills. It is therefore important that you carefully select where your athletes gather

for the introduction. For example, when teaching rebounding in basketball, it makes sense to meet near the key. Likewise, to teach an inbounds pass, you need to be near a sideline. Positional cues add meaning to the demonstration.

Formations

Your most important concern when you arrange a demonstration is making sure that all team members can see the demonstrator. We suggest using the formations illustrated in chapter 2. In addition don't hesitate to adjust the formations by asking athletes to move to where they can see the demonstration clearly.

Regardless of the formation you select, however, be certain that all your athletes can watch the performance from the same angle. For example, if you stand too close to the team while using a semicircle formation, the athletes on the ends of the formation will be watching a side view of your demonstration, which might prevent them from seeing clearly the points you are making in your explanation. Picture teaching a golf swing in such a formation: By aligning yourself so that those in the middle of the semicircle see a side view of the demonstration, athletes at the ends will see a front or rear view, both of which are highly ineffective.

In fact, standing too close to any formation can become a serious problem because many of your athletes may be shielded from seeing the things you are emphasizing in your explanation. If the majority of your athletes cannot see all of the important aspects of a demonstration, you should move the demonstrator to a more advantageous position; if only one or two athletes are unable to observe clearly, ask them to move.

Viewpoints

If your athletes are able to see all the important aspects of the skill from a single viewing angle, organize the demonstration from only one angle. Most skills, however, are best presented from more than one angle. For example, the demonstrator can present the skill of basketball dribbling from the side, looking in the same direction as the athletes, or facing them. Each direction allows the players to notice a different aspect of the skill. The front view illustrates the contribution of the hands, face, and eyes; and facing the same way as the athletes presents a model of the skill from the player's perspective.

Front and Side Views

To illustrate further, suppose you are coaching wrestling and want to introduce beginning wrestlers to the proper stance. You could first demonstrate the front view of the stance and then change positions to demonstrate the side view. As you can see in Figure 4.1, the front view enables the wrestlers to note the distance between the arms, the space between the feet, and the upper body position, centered between the feet. From the side view the wrestlers can see that the back is straight, how far the right foot is behind the left foot, the position of the upper body relative to the feet, and how much the elbows are bending. This information would be very difficult to convey with an explanation. The figure illustrates the importance of a visual representation of the skill.

Figure 4.1 Two views of a wrestling stance.

Using Mirrors

In some situations the athletes, rather than the demonstrator, may have to change positions to obtain the best viewing angle for a live demonstration. This is especially true when the environment determines how the skill is performed, such as gymnastic skills on the parallel bars. Utilizing mirrors in your demonstration is one way to get around problems set by equipment limitations. However, be sure to tell your athletes when they are to watch the demonstrator and when they should look at

the mirror. Mirrors can also be useful when you want to emphasize having the athletes imitate a certain form or technique, such as a baseball batting stance and swing or a golf stance and swing. Figure 4.2 illustrates examples of such an arrangement.

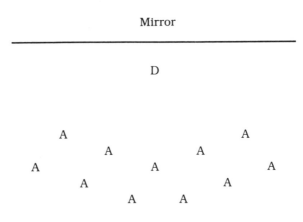

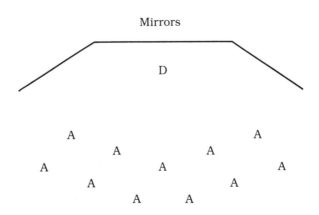

Figure 4.2 Two ways to use mirrors to demonstrate a skill. D = demonstrator and A = Athlete

Facing Toward or Away From Athletes

Some skills demonstrations are difficult for athletes to watch when the demonstrator is facing them. Trying to do the opposite of what you see can be confusing, especially for the young player. If you are familiar with the backhand return in tennis, you'll know that two teaching points to emphasize are the footwork involved in a backhand pivot and the change required to go from a forehand grip of the racquet to a backhand grip. These are shown in Figure 4.3.

Same Viewing Angle

Opposite Viewing Angle

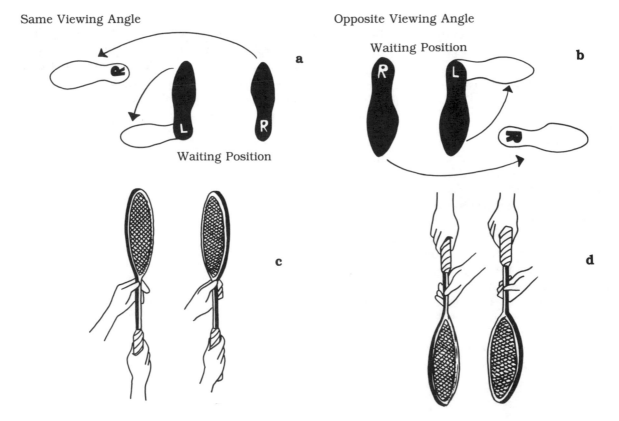

Figure 4.3 Foot position and grip for backhand return in tennis from the same-facing and opposite viewing angles. Use the following instructions: Turn the racquet slightly to the right with your left hand. Then, tighten your grip again with your right hand, remove your left hand.

Try performing the footwork for the backhand pivot while facing the same direction as your players (viewing angle shown in part *a*). The coach moves the right foot across the body from the ready position, and the athletes simply follow. Now try the opposite viewing angle (shown in part *b*). The coach is facing the athlete while moving the right foot across the left foot; the athlete sees a foot moving from left to right. This can cause confusion. Now look at parts *c* and *d* and decide which way is easier for learning to change from the forehand to the backhand grip.

This problem becomes more acute when you want your athletes to follow along with a demonstration, such as practicing guarding a person dribbling in basketball. The athlete's left side is the same as your right side, and he or she may easily become confused by references to left and right. Similar problems sometimes occur when whole activities are taught by demonstration. When teaching calisthenics or aerobic exercises, for example, have you or your athletes become confused between your left and right side and their left and right side? When teaching these activities the most

effective method is to stand with your back to the class and allow them to imitate you.

You may decide that it is unwise to face away from the group when coaching young athletes because from this position you are unable to see how your athletes are copying your movement. An alternative strategy is to face the group and perform the skill in the same direction the group is moving—that is, to present a mirror image. In the tennis backhand example your explanation would remain the same, but you would move your left foot across your right. Following this procedure, you and the athletes would be facing the same direction as you turn.

The Performer's Viewpoint

Presenting a skill from the same viewing angle that the performer sees during execution can sometimes be the only way a particular cue or component is visible. Videotapes that give this viewing angle can be particularly beneficial aids—the athletes see exactly what they will see during performance. This strategy would be very useful, for example, in downhill skiing because it would help the skier learn when and where to start making the next turn. Another such sport is rifle shooting. Figure 4.4 shows the sight picture of a rifle shooter who is using a hood as a front sight with an aperture insert and having a small disc with a small hole in it as the rear sight. Having novice

Figure 4.4 Sight picture for a rifle shooter using a hood as a front sight with an aperture insert and a small disc with a small hole in it as the rear sight.

shooters study this sight picture will give them an idea of what they should be seeing as they take aim at a target.

Imagine the advantage a football coach would have in teaching checkoff points to a middle linebacker by using films of what the player could actually see. This type of videotape seems easy enough to produce if a coach is creative. Are there skills in your sport that lend themselves to demonstration from a performer's viewpoint? Consider developing pictures or videos that provide the information for your athletes.

A Final Word

Before you break up your demonstration formation, be sure to arrange your athletes to practice the skill. Remember, like your demonstration formation, practice formations should be simple, easy to move to, easily monitored, and safe. In addition, the best practice situations provide a great deal of athlete involvement and activity.

We once observed a basketball coach trying to teach his athletes how to line up to receive an inbounds pass. They sat on the gym floor while he explained on the blackboard what he wanted done. He then told them to find a practice area and to try inbounding the ball. The result was chaos because his athletes were unable to transfer the information presented on the blackboard into the practice setting—they had no idea where to go or who should be doing what.

Consider, however, a very different approach for teaching the inbounds pass as practiced by Coach Jones. First he organized his athletes into six groups of four and numbered each athlete either 1, 2, 3, or 4. He then took one of the groups and said the following: "Number 1 will inbound, Number 2 will receive the ball, Number 3 will defend Number 1, and Number 4 will defend Number 2. I want Number 2 to move and try to lose the defender." Next, he organized a demonstration of how the drill should be performed and walked a group of athletes through the drill several times to make sure that they knew who was to receive the ball and who was covering whom. He then sent each group to a specific area of the gymnasium and had them get into their assigned positions before signaling for practice to begin. The result was a practice in which all of the athletes knew exactly where to go and what to do.

WHO SHOULD DEMONSTRATE?

Selecting the most appropriate individual or group of individuals to perform the demonstration will have a major impact on the effectiveness of the demonstration. When organizing demonstrations, you have several options for choosing who will perform them. These include live demonstrations—by yourself, your assistants, your athletes, and invited performers—and recorded performances on film and video tape. When making your choice, consider the skill level of your athletes. How well can one or more of them demonstrate the skill or strategy? In addition, what kind of cues do your athletes respond to? What is your own skill level and that of your assistant coaches? Finally what is the availability of resources like films, videos, and other expert performers?

Similarity of Models

When demonstrating skills to beginners, try to use a demonstrator who is able to perform the skill correctly and is respected by your athletes. Ideally, your demonstrator should be the same gender as your athletes as well as the same size and physical maturity. Thus your athletes will be able to identify with the demonstrator and believe that they can learn to perform the skill too. Regardless of whom you choose, however, be sure that the demonstration shows, and that you emphasize in the explanation, the specific teaching points you want to make. This is sometimes difficult to arrange, especially when coaching beginning athletes: Too often, only a few athletes at this stage will have the ability to demonstrate a new skill successfully.

One method of overcoming some of these limitations is to arrange for a few of the athletes to come to practice several minutes early. Run through the different demonstrations you use in the practice and make sure that the athletes can perform the demonstrations exactly as you want. Rehearsal of the skill increases the confidence of the demonstrators. Consequently, the demonstrations run smoothly, and the athletes' confidence is boosted because they have seen their teammates perform the desired skills. To avoid charges of favoritism, take care to select different athletes for each day's demonstrations. Of course, this requires that you *plan ahead*.

Coach as a Model

When coaches choose to demonstrate, it's essential that they perform the skills correctly. Effective demonstrations give athletes confidence in their coach, but poor demonstrations have the reverse effect. It is not, however, important that you be perfect. Missing a free throw when you are demonstrating does *not* mean your demonstration was ineffective; it only means that you, too, can miss a shot. Your demonstration would, however, be ineffective if you missed the shot because you did not perform the skill correctly from a technical standpoint.

Some Ideas

If you are not confident about your ability to execute a technically correct demonstration, either practice the demonstration yourself beforehand or arrange for another person to demonstrate. Consider inviting a young athlete to your practice who has acquired the skill you intend to teach. This may turn out to be a more effective strategy than demonstrating yourself because your athletes will see that the skill can be performed by someone near their own age.

During the practice look for opportunities to use group members for demonstrations. When an athlete does something well, stop practice and have that athlete demonstrate in front of the others. Provided the coach gives different athletes the chance to demonstrate, this strategy boosts the confidence of the performer and motivates others in the group to try even harder.

For Advanced Athletes

It is often more difficult to arrange live demonstrations for highly skilled athletes because they can frequently perform some skills better than the coaching staff or the rest of the team. In these instances use invited experts or films and videos of athletes who are more skilled than your athletes and who are well known for their exemplary technique. However, be sure that you select demonstrations with which your athletes can identify. Ideally, for example, gymnastic demonstrations should feature performers similar to your athletes in body build, maturational age, and gender. The techniques of a muscular, short-limbed athlete can be quite different from those of a taller and less muscular athlete. Of course, such models are not always available, but coaches should strive to find demonstrators who are as similar as possible to their athletes.

The same is also true in many other sports. Consider Kareem Abdul Jabbar's skyhook, one of the most famous moves in basketball and one of the reasons Jabbar became the all-time leading scorer in the National Basketball Association. When Jabbar is playing at his best, the shot is almost impossible to defend.

This is partly because of his tremendous skill but also due to the fact that he is 7 feet 2 inches tall. To teach your basketball players how to perform the skyhook, a technically sound demonstration performed by a player the same size as your players would probably be more informative than watching Jabbar perform the same shot.

Demonstrations can also be an important method for refining skills. Advanced athletes who have learned complete skills benefit from demonstrations aimed at changing one or more particular aspects of the skill. For example, a slalom skier might be initiating the turn too late. The coach could demonstrate correct technique on one turn, even to an advanced skier. Thus the coach could demonstrate a key element of the skill without repeating the entire performance. Coaching advanced athletes presents many opportunities of this type. Being unable to clear 19-plus feet in the pole vault does not disqualify you from demonstrating key parts of the skill, like the hand position at the plant. At every coaching level, you must distinguish between proficiently demonstrating part of the skill and demonstrating the whole skill.

USING FILM OR VIDEO DEMONSTRATIONS AND SOUND AS A MODEL

In recent years audiovisual aids have become less expensive, easier to use, and more readily available. Films and videos are valuable for both introducing and demonstrating new skills as well as for analyzing performance problems.

Advantages of Films and Videos for Demonstrating Skills

The advantages of film and video demonstration include the following:

- The athletes can view and review the same demonstration as many times as is necessary.
- The skill can be demonstrated from many different angles, some of which cannot be seen in live demonstrations. For example, in many team sports a view from directly above can provide assistance with team formations and strategies.
- The film or video can be speeded up, slowed down, or stopped to examine a skill or parts of a skill in more detail.
- You can focus on one particular aspect of the skill.

Disadvantages of Films and Videos for Demonstrating Skills

The disadvantages of film and video models include the following:

- Film and video require expensive equipment and a knowledgeable operator.
- It is difficult to show films and videos out of doors, although this is becoming less of a problem with the introduction of small, portable equipment.
- A film is less personal and does not convey depth and distance as well as a live demonstration.
- Despite their potential versatility, film and videotape seldom include all the angles that you want to present.
- Filming and then showing the filmed or videotaped demonstration takes considerable time.

Using Slow Motion for Demonstrations

Before using slow-motion films or videos, always show the demonstration at its normal speed. It's important for athletes initially to appreciate the speed at which the skill is to be performed in competition. The advantage of slow-motion replay is that it will permit you to focus on one particular aspect of the performance and enable you to direct your athletes to concentrate on this specific point. Once your athletes have understood what you want them to do, show the demonstration one more time at the correct speed, then have your athletes practice the skill.

Using Still Pictures for Demonstrations

Showing your athletes still pictures can be another effective way of demonstrating skills. However, for most skills still pictures are best used in conjunction with a live demonstration, video, or film demonstration of the skill performed at normal game speed. A major limitation of still pictures is that they do not teach the timing of the whole skill. Nevertheless, they remain useful for displaying detailed points of technique at a particular moment, such as the proper positioning of the parts of the body in relation to each other.

Still pictures are ideally suited for showing the relationship between a sport implement, such as racquet or baseball bat, and the athlete's body. For example, pictures can be used to show how tennis players need to keep the racquet head higher than their wrist. They can also depict the relationship of teammates and opponents. As an example, the picture in Figure 4.5 shows the proper positioning of the goalkeeper and the areas of the net to be protected in ice hockey.

Still pictures are also valuable for isolating key positions during a movement sequence.

Figure 4.6 is a sequence of illustrations of a baseball swing. The figure notes the correct position of the body and its parts relative to the baseball bat and ball at different times during the swing.

Figure 4.6   A sequential view of the baseball swing.

Finally, still pictures can be useful for showing close-ups that cannot normally be seen in a typical demonstration. Figure 4.7 displays a close-up picture of the grip used to hold a golf club; the grip cannot be seen clearly when the swing is being demonstrated.

Figure 4.5   Areas of net protected by the goalkeeper.

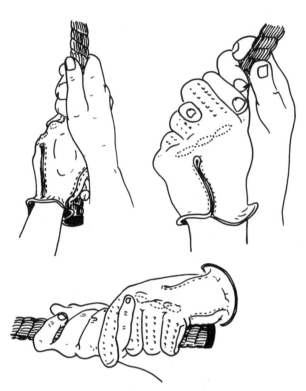

Figure 4.7 Three different views of how to grip a golf club.

Remember that still pictures supplement but do not replace live, videotape, and film demonstrations of skills performed at normal speed. Use them to make charts for wall displays or show them as slides or overhead transparencies in conjunction with a live demonstration. Another idea that some coaches have found helpful is to make copies of pictures that illustrate key points of technique and distribute them to team members for review at home between practice sessions.

Using Sound as a Model

Imagine that you are teaching your long jumpers to triple jump, and they all have achieved a reasonable skill level. However, one of your athletes is taking a long hop, a very short step, and a medium-length jump. How can you help your athlete equalize the length of the hop, step, and jump? Are there any demonstrations or models you can use?

Visual demonstrations of how to break the triple jump into components will obviously

help. You could mark the ground at three equal places and have your athletes practice landing on each mark. You could then adjust the marks to optimize performance. In addition, you could either videotape the athlete or present an example of an athlete performing correctly.

An alternative approach would be to record the sound of a correct performance and compare it to your athlete's performance. The correct pattern would have four relatively equally spaced sounds, whereas the athlete you're coaching would have a long gap between the first and second sound, a short gap between the second and third, and a long gap between the third and fourth. Comparing the two sound patterns would provide valuable feedback for your athlete. The sound model would also be beneficial in assisting the athlete to develop the appropriate timing pattern.

OTHER FACTORS TO CONSIDER BEFORE GIVING A DEMONSTRATION

At least three other factors should be considered before you demonstrate a skill. Ask yourself the following questions:

- How often should the skill be demonstrated?
- Does the skill have to be broken down into parts to be demonstrated effectively?
- Does the skill need to be demonstrated with each limb?

How Often Should the Skill Be Demonstrated?

The number of times a skill needs to be demonstrated depends on the complexity of the skill in relation to the ability of your athletes. A simple skill, such as the two-handed chest pass in basketball, may require only one or two demonstrations, but a more complex skill, like the front-crawl in swimming, will need several demonstrations of the whole stroke as well as many demonstrations of the parts.

For demonstrating different team plays and their options, several demonstrations are advised. During the first demonstration you should mention one or two cues for your athletes to look for, and you should be prepared to add others during subsequent demonstrations. If you are introducing a complex skill, supplement the initial demonstration with additional demonstrations and cues throughout the practice phase. But choose the proper time for these additional demonstrations—when your athletes are becoming tired or frustrated, a short break and change of pace may help improve their performance.

When in doubt about how many demonstrations to give, it is better to give too many than too few. If you give too many demonstrations, the only risk you run is boring some of your athletes. However, at least you will know that they understand what you want them to do. If you give them too few demonstrations, on the other hand, the athletes may not understand what you want them to practice and may experience repeated failures.

Does the Skill Need to be Broken Down Into Parts to Be Demonstrated Effectively?

If some of your athletes fail to repeat a demonstration, it may be because the skill was too complicated for them to understand. In these situations your athletes may learn the skill more effectively if it can be broken down into smaller parts. You should remember that in the previous chapter we introduced the concept of subdividing skills into three stages: the preparation, the action, and the completion. You may need to demonstrate each of the stages.

There are two additional considerations influencing skills for demonstration purposes. First, if a skill has parts that can be performed in isolation, they can also be demonstrated in isolation. For example, all swimming strokes can be subdivided into the arm action, the leg action, and breathing. If each aspect is demonstrated separately, your athletes need only concentrate on one aspect at a time. The risk of presenting skills in this manner is that your athletes will not see the relationship between the different parts and be unable to learn the timing of the stroke. Fortunately, this problem

can usually be overcome if you demonstrate the whole skill first and then demonstrate each part.

A second principle to follow is analyzing the skill to decide how many key points there are. If there are more key points than your athletes' memory span can handle, consider breaking the skill down further. Those of you who have played tennis will know that the tennis serve can be broken down into many parts, including foot position, ball toss, racquet swing, and follow-through—and each of these parts contains further subdivisions. Effective tennis coaches would probably demonstrate the whole skill at the outset of learning so that their athletes could see the entire skill and the interrelationship between the parts; they would then demonstrate each part separately, highlighting the important cues.

Does the Skill Need to be Demonstrated With Each Limb?

Do you need to consider limb preference when teaching your athletes new sport skills? If so, remember to begin your instruction by asking them their preferred side to perform the skill. For example, do they prefer to spike the volleyball with their right or left hand? You might find that each of your athletes has a right side preference, in which case you need not initially demonstrate from the left side. When you have athletes with a mixture of preferences, plan to demonstrate from both sides.

In many sports, however, it is beneficial and sometimes essential to be able to use both limbs with equal effectiveness. Soccer players, for example, quickly learn to force opponents toward one side of the field if the player can dribble with only one foot. In basketball, similarly, defending against an athlete who can dribble with either hand is more difficult. Even in track and field, there are instances when it is beneficial to use either leg equally well. In both the intermediate hurdles and the steeplechase, it is much more efficient to hurdle without changing stride. This can be done most easily if your athletes can hurdle off either leg. When you want your athletes to practice with both limbs, arrange for the practice to be preceded with a demonstration by an athlete using both limbs.

Demonstration Evaluation Form

In the column at the left, indicate the most appropriate number for each item as follows: 1 = *no* and 2 = *yes*.

1. _____ Directs the team's attention to the demonstration.
2. _____ Athletes are arranged so that everyone can see the demonstration.
3. _____ Demonstrates the whole skill as it would be performed in competition.
4. _____ Demonstrates skillfully.
5. _____ Demonstrates for left-handers as well as right-handers.
6. _____ Demonstrates the skill an adequate number of times.
7. _____ Demonstrates the skill so that it is viewed from different angles.
8. _____ Demonstrates the skill at a slower speed if necessary.
9. _____ Points out the major sequence of actions that constitute the skill when it is demonstrated at a slow speed.
10. _____ Demonstrates parts of the skill if appropriate.
11. _____ Demonstrates similarities and differences between the new skill and previously learned skills that are related.
12. _____ Demonstrates the most relevant cues.

Add up your 12 ratings and write the total score here: _____. Compare your score with the results listed below to determine how effectively you presented your demonstration.

> 22–24 = **superior**
> 19–21 = **above average**
> 16–18 = **average**
> 13–15 = **below average**
> 12 = **inferior**

EVALUATING YOUR DEMONSTRATION

As with introducing and explaining, merely demonstrating a skill is not enough. You need to evaluate your experiences to determine how effective you were. You can do this by having yourself videotaped while you are demonstrating a new skill to your athletes. If that is not possible, have one of your assistant coaches observe your demonstration and evaluate it using the evaluation form above.

SUMMARY AND RECOMMENDATIONS

Demonstrations are the most effective means of giving your athletes the idea of what you want them to learn. Accompany your demonstration with a brief explanation identifying what you want your athletes to concentrate on. To achieve the highest rate of learning from your demonstrations, make sure that your athletes (a) watch and attend to the demonstration, (b) understand what you want them to do, (c) have the ability to perform the skill, and (d) are motivated.

Keep the following points in mind as you plan your demonstrations.

1. Arrange your demonstrations so that all of your athletes can see.
2. Consider using demonstrations not only at the beginning but also during and at the end of practice for a particular skill.
3. Use your assistants, your athletes, other athletes, films and videos, and yourself to perform the demonstrations.

4. The best person to act as demonstrator is an athlete as much like the athletes you are coaching as possible.
5. Use films and videos whenever possible.
6. Use slow motion to concentrate on aspects of performance that are difficult to follow at normal speed.
7. Use still pictures in conjunction with demonstrations for illustrating hard-to-see points of technique and for composing wall displays and handouts.
8. Always demonstrate the whole skill first and then demonstrate different parts.
9. Give demonstrations as often as necessary.
10. Give the demonstration from the best viewing angle for that particular skill.
11. If appropriate, have your models use both right and left limbs.
12. After the demonstration check that all your athletes have understood the demonstration. If they have not, repeat and clarify.
13. Evaluate your effectiveness at presenting demonstrations.

Chapter 5
Helping Athletes Attempt Difficult Skills

In chapters 3 and 4 you read about how to introduce, explain, and demonstrate skills to your athletes. This chapter will discuss how you can assist them in their efforts to reproduce the skills you are teaching.

After your introduction, explanation, and demonstration, your athletes should have a good idea of the skill being taught and should be ready to begin practicing it. Be sure that the practice formation you select is simple to understand, easy to move through, and appropriate for practicing the skill you are presenting. It should allow the greatest number of your athletes to practice the skill safely and effectively. At the same time, the formation should facilitate your ability to observe and evaluate your athletes' performance and to provide them with corrective and encouraging feedback. Regardless of the type of formation you choose, of course, be certain that you briefly explain and demonstrate how it will operate and answer all relevant questions so that everyone understands how to proceed.

Once practice is under way, use the following guidelines to evaluate its effectiveness:

1. Note whether or not most of your athletes are making a sincere, well-motivated effort to perform the skill as it was explained and demonstrated.
2. Identify the parts of the skill that most of your athletes are performing correctly and incorrectly.
3. Analyze the cause of the errors and determine what you will say when you are making corrections.
4. Select no more than one or two errors to correct at a time; trying to do more can cause undue confusion.

When you are properly prepared, stop the practice, get your athletes' attention, and provide feedback that is appropriate for the entire team. Use a positive approach:

- If they are making an effort, compliment your athletes on their attempts to perform the skill.
- Compliment them on the parts of their performance they have executed correctly.
- Briefly explain and, if appropriate, demonstrate how the skill was executed incorrectly; then briefly explain and demonstrate how to correct the error.
- Make sure that your athletes understand the corrections you have presented before you permit them to attempt the skill again.
- Encourage your athletes to make the corrections you suggested and have them make several attempts to perform the skill again.

After common errors have been corrected, begin working with one athlete at a time to help refine his or her performance. Chapters 8 and 9 discuss the techniques you will need.

Presumably your athletes will not be able to perform all skills effectively on the first attempt. Many will make major errors, and some may resist attempting a new and difficult skill, particularly if it is somewhat complex and/or involves risk of injury. Skills of this type might include, for example, the handstand in gymnastics or diving off a diving board into a swimming pool. When you are confronting this situation, your task is much more difficult than usual. Nevertheless, the key points discussed in this chapter will help you assist your athletes in learning to perform skills at all levels of difficulty. The following list is an outline of these points:

- Repeating the instructional process
- Using *part* methods
- Minimizing fear of injury
- Minimizing fear of failure

REPEATING THE INSTRUCTIONAL PROCESS

Repeating the instructional process is a very effective technique for helping a group of athletes perform a skill they are having difficulty executing at the outset of learning. In fact, many coaches report that the first thing they do when their athletes can't perform a skill is repeat the instructional process. Although variations of the process are possible, it consists essentially of four steps.

1. *Provide feedback to your athletes.* After you have stopped the practice and the team is paying attention, compliment your athletes for their effort to perform the skill and provide plenty of encouragement. Thereafter, offer appropriate information to help them correct their performance errors.
2. *Repeat the explanation and demonstration.* If your corrections are not helping your athletes to perform the skill effectively, repeat the explanation and demonstration. You might consider performing the skill more slowly than you did before or stopping at critical points during the demonstration to emphasize the most relevant cues.
3. *Verify your athletes' understanding.* One way to be sure that your corrections and further demonstrations are being understood is to ask the team to repeat the information you presented; another technique is to question them to verify their understanding. Of course, don't forget to answer relevant questions they may have about the information presented.
4. *Let your athletes try the skill again.* At this point have your athletes attempt to perform the skill again. If you see

only moderate progress, you may need to repeat one or more of the first three steps. However, if you observe no progress whatsoever, you may have to use another procedure (see the following sections) or go on to something else in the practice. Several factors can prevent progress: You may be trying to teach a skill that, unmodified, is too complex for the level of development of your athletes; you may be teaching the skill incorrectly. In any case, review the situation after practice and consider discussing it with your assistant coaches or even a few of the athletes. This approach may give you insight into why the skill was so difficult to perform and what might be done to resolve the problem.

USING PART METHODS

When you decide that a skill in its entirety is too complex for your athletes to master at the outset of learning, divide it into its component parts and teach each one separately. Demonstrate and explain the first part of the skill you want them to learn and have them attempt to perform it. If they succeed, have them practice that portion of the skill before introducing the next component. Then demonstrate, explain, and practice the remaining parts according to the steps outlined in chapter 7. Regardless of the method you use, however, if you use it properly, your athletes will eventually be able to perform the whole skill.

Let's look at an example. A diving coach uses the part method in teaching a twisting somersault dive. Part 1 of the skill is the takeoff, Part 2 is the somersault, and Part 3 is the twist. Moreover, the individual parts can be subdivided further if fear of injury becomes a problem. In fact, teaching the parts separately seems to make it easier for the divers to put all of their concerns behind them.

An added advantage of teaching skills by the part method is that it gives athletes more opportunity to experience success. The more success they experience, the more confidence they are likely to build, and confidence is an important key to successful athletic performance.

USING GUIDANCE TECHNIQUES

Many athletes will begin to develop the desired motor program if they are guided through the movement sequence. You can provide several types of guidance: (a) visual, (b) verbal, (c) combined visual and verbal, and (d) manual.

Visual Guidance

Providing visual guidance means that you instruct your athletes to do what they *see* you do. This assumes, of course, that you are able to perform the skill being presented. This method of guidance is similar to playing follow-the-leader and can be an effective strategy when teaching very young athletes.

You will usually be facing in the same direction as the group and demonstrating the skill step-by-step. You should proceed through the demonstration as slowly as possible so that the athletes can get a clear view and imitate each step immediately after they see it. You should be certain that each step is being imitated correctly. If errors occur, provide feedback to correct them, then repeat the corrected step and continue. Many coaches include this strategy in their regular teaching procedures for complex skills.

Verbal Guidance

Using verbal guidance is similar to a game of Simon-Says. Ask your athletes to do exactly what they *hear* you say they should do. You are, in fact, providing them with a label for the movements they need to make, so your cues must be simple and clear, although they may be either literal or figurative.

For example, in teaching a backward roll to elementary school children, one coach uses the following labels: bunny ears, roll, and push. The labels correspond to the hand positions necessary for leverage to perform the roll: beginning position (bunny ears), rolling across the back (roll), and extending the arms (push) to roll over the head to the feet. Notice that the cues are simple, clear, and meaningful to the children.

Simply providing labels is insufficient, however. You must also observe and evaluate the performances of your athletes. If you notice gross errors, suggest a correction using alternative labels and have your athletes repeat their performance.

If you are dividing the skill into parts, label each part, practice the segment until it is performed properly and then move on to the next. When each of the parts has been learned, you can string them together. In addition, you may ask your athletes to practice very complex skills more slowly than they would ordinarily be performed, but remember that this is not practical for some skills, especially if they involve working against gravity. In that case, slower movements require that you provide additional support, which will be discussed later. Whatever the complexity involved, however, be sure that your athletes attempt to perform the skill at the speed at which it should be performed as soon as they are able.

Verbal pretraining (described in chapter 3) is an effective way of combining labels for complex skills in which timing is important. The athlete can rehearse the sequence verbally before performing the skill rather than using the labels while the skill is being performed.

Combining Visual and Verbal Guidance

This approach could also be called show-and-tell. To use this method, demonstrate (show) the first part of the skill, provide simple labels (tell) that will help the athletes generate the desired movement, and immediately have the group attempt to perform the part. As each part is mastered, move on to the next one until all parts can be performed correctly. At this point you can demonstrate the entire skill while using the labels, then ask your athletes to attempt the skill.

Manual Guidance

Have you ever seen a parent standing behind a child helping him or her swing a baseball bat? That parent is providing manual guidance. To use this teaching method in your practices, tell the athlete to relax and let you do most of the work. You will move him or her through the desired movement sequence. Ask the athlete to concentrate on how the skill *feels* while being guided through the movement. After several repetitions with manual guidance, ask for a performance of the skill without your assistance. Manual guidance is also quite useful for correcting errors, but be sure to ask the athlete to attempt to perform the skill without your assistance as soon as the guided correction is complete.

Although manual guidance can be effective when working with a small number of athletes, it is not recommended for a large group. The time spent moving from athlete to athlete guiding them through a skill can be excessive, and the athletes waiting for attention can become bored. Moreover, if your whole team is having great difficulty learning a skill, consider whether or not your athletes are ready to learn this particular skill and review your progression through introduction, explanation, and demonstration.

MINIMIZING FEAR OF INJURY

Before young athletes will attempt to perform a skill that has an inherent element of danger or risk, they need to be convinced that they will not get hurt when they attempt to perform

the skill. Remember, however, that you can destroy an athlete's sport career and open yourself to a lawsuit if you don't take the necessary safety precautions. You can minimize both risk and fear of injury by

- using logically designed skill progressions,
- demonstrating and explaining that they are ready (capable) to perform the skill,
- modifying the conditions under which the skill is typically performed to eliminate the perceived danger, and
- teaching your athletes the safety maneuvers related to the sport skill before they learn the skill.

Progressions

Progression is a key consideration when introducing athletes to skills involving physical contact. Most athletes naturally feel frightened at the prospect of physical contact when playing sports like football, wrestling, and ice hockey. Similarly, some children will fear putting their face in the water, which will need to be overcome before they can learn to swim successfully. In a swimming situation you might gradually progress from splashing in the water to washing the face to playing games like ring-around-the-rosie to reaching for brightly colored objects on the pool floor. Moving slowly through the stages often helps children overcome their initial fears. By considering the potential fears of your athletes carefully, you should be able to develop your progressions to ensure as much success as possible.

Readiness

Assuring your athletes that they possess the necessary prerequisite skills, strength, and flexibility to perform a skill will also go a long way toward convincing them that it is safe to attempt the skill. If you have planned your teaching approach for the entire season according to the suggestions in chapter 1 of this book and chapter 8 of *Coaching Young Athletes* (Martens et al., 1981), you will have prepared your athletes well to learn the skills you are about to present. Explaining the planning process to your athletes and expressing confidence in their abilities are often helpful ways to instill a sense of readiness.

Skill Modification

In addition to the previous suggestions, you can often change the conditions under which the skill is usually performed. A handstand, for example, is normally performed away from all obstructions and support. Athletes attempting the handstand for the first time may be fearful of kicking the legs up too forcefully and overbalancing, which can cause a hard, painful landing on the back. They may also be afraid of

- collapsing onto a hard floor and hitting the head if unable to support the body weight or
- falling to either the right or the left.

However, by changing the conditions for performance—adding supports and other safety features—you can remove many of these fears.

A coach could modify the practice conditions so that the handstand is performed (a) on a mat or with some other soft material beneath the performer's head, (b) with a teammate serving as a spotter, or (c) against a wall. Having a mat beneath the head will reduce the fear of falling to the floor and hitting one's head. A spotter standing to one side of the youngster performing the handstand can help reduce the athlete's chances of falling right or left by controlling the performer's legs with his or her hands. Doing a handstand against the wall eliminates the possibility of falling over

backwards and hurting the back. Utilizing modified practice conditions allows you to demonstrate and explain the skill and to emphasize the additional precautions taken to ensure the athletes' safety.

Safety Procedures

Using spotters to modify practice, as just described will not work, of course, unless you teach spotting techniques to all the team members. Furthermore, each athlete must develop confidence in the spotters with whom he or she is working. Such procedures are standard on most gymnastics teams. Diving teams also use support techniques extensively. Hand spotting and using spotting belts are common. Practicing use of modified techniques, however, should not continue for a prolonged period of time because your athletes may become too dependent on the extra support and their performance may suffer. As your athletes become more competent, you should systematically remove the extra safety and guidance factors and replace them with more routine safety measures and instruction. Remember, additional safety measures are designed to give your athletes confidence and physical support when they first perform a skill or perform a new and complex skill for the first time. After working through a series of progressions, your athletes will gradually develop the confidence to attempt the skill without any additional support.

Contact Sport Procedures

For contact sports a similar procedure should be followed. Your responsibility as coach is to provide a progression of steps leading up to full contact and to be sure that your athletes are ready for contact. You need to modify practice conditions to minimize fear of contact injury. For example, a coach might begin teaching tackling in football by (a) walking the athletes through the technique and emphasizing form, (b) working at walking pace with a partner, (c) tackling at 60% speed with a tackling dummy, (d) tackling at 100% speed with a dummy, (e) tackling at 60% against a partner, and, finally, (f) working at 100% with a partner. Such a progression is intended to introduce your athletes gradually to the type of contact they will experience as they participate in their sport. It should reduce unrealistic fears of injury and help to instill confidence.

MINIMIZING FEAR OF FAILURE

Some athletes do not perform the skill reasonably well after the demonstration–explanation because they are afraid of making gross performance errors. They often believe that their performance of a skill is an important indicator of their value as human beings. If they perform the skill well, they consider themselves worthy, but if they perform poorly, they see themselves as bad or worthless.

This attitude is an unfortunate distortion of the reality of mastering sport skills. The negative thinking that accompanies labeling a poor performance as a failure and attributing worthlessness to the athlete is, of course, detrimental to learning a skill. Statements like "I'm no good" or "I can't do anything right" can make athletes apprehensive about even trying to perform a skill. If athletes remain thus confused about skill performance, they may be programming themselves for failure.

You are responsible to ensure that your athletes avoid this type of negative thinking. Throughout the season you must discourage behavior reflecting this unrealistic attitude, such as ridiculing a fellow teammate for making an obvious error. Be careful that *you* present a positive attitude toward your athletes, especially when they make errors. Remind your athletes that errors are a natural part of the learning process and should not be confused with their worth as human beings. Errors are inevitable especially early in learning. Therefore, athletes must learn to expect them to occur and, further realize that errors actually contribute to improving performance. Viewed in this way, errors serve as the stepping-stones to achievement. (You will find more information on how to enhance an athlete's feelings of worthiness in the *Coaches Guide to Sport Psychology* [Martens, 1987].)

SUMMARY AND RECOMMENDATIONS

After you have presented a new skill, some of your athletes will be able to perform the skill well enough to begin practicing it. In this situation your job is to provide feedback to them during practice. You should reinforce what they are doing correctly and then comment on major errors widespread among team members. You may find it necessary to conduct additional demonstrations. As your athletes become more proficient, you can turn your attention to each athlete and attempt to improve his or her performance.

Many athletes have a difficult time performing a complex skill when it is first presented to them. You have a variety of options for helping them achieve successful performance:

1. Repeat the instructional process, which consists of providing usefully corrective feedback, repeating the explanation-demonstration slowly and carefully, checking your athletes' understanding, and letting them try the skill again.
2. Use part methods of teaching a complex skill.
3. Use visual, verbal, and manual guidance techniques or a combination of them to help your athletes get the general idea of how to perform the skill.
4. Carefully plan seasonal skill progressions so that athletes have mastered prerequisite skills before attempting the new skill.
5. Modify learning conditions to minimize fear of injury.
6. Emphasize encouragement and promote a positive atmosphere on your team; view athletes' errors as positive, necessary steps in the skill-learning process.
7. Minimize fear of failure by creating an atmosphere in which errors are viewed as a natural part of practicing rather than as indicators of human worth.

PART III
Developing and Maintaining Skills

Once your athletes are able to perform a skill well enough to begin practicing it, you will be responsible for teaching them to develop (learn) the skill to their highest level of proficiency. After the skill is highly developed, you will need to help your athletes maintain their skill level by teaching them to retain (remember) what they have learned. The specific ways in which you can teach your athletes and design conditions for them to develop and maintain their skills is what part 3 of this book is all about!

In chapter 6 you will learn about the variables influencing the effectiveness of practice. You will find this information very useful when you design your practice conditions throughout the season. In chapter 7 we will tell

you how to make complex skills easier for your athletes to learn. This information will be very helpful when you are faced with teaching your athletes skills that are difficult to learn. The use and operation of feedback in the teaching and learning of skills will be discussed in chapter 8. Understanding how feedback functions is a prerequisite for using it effectively in your teaching. In chapter 9 you will learn how to analyze your athletes' skill performance and use a positive approach in correcting their errors. The information in this chapter will help you to evaluate your athletes' performance, determine what needs to be corrected, and then effectively communicate your corrections to them.

Chapter 6
Variables Influencing Effectiveness of Practice

No athlete ever learned to hit a baseball, swim the crawl stroke, juggle a soccer ball, dribble a basketball, or perform a handstand merely by watching someone else or by practicing the skills mentally. Observation and mental practice may be very helpful, but the only way learning takes place is by physically practicing the skill with the intent to improve while receiving useful feedback. Without the intent to improve, practice can lead to a mediocre level of skill proficiency or, worse, a deterioration of skill level. Consider for a moment your own handwriting. Once long ago you had little proficiency in handwriting skills. When handwriting was taught in school—with physical practice and appropriate feedback, among other things—you reached a certain level of proficiency. As a result of your self-directed practice, have you regressed a little, leveled off to a mediocre level, or entered the realm of the barely legible?

In the competitive world of sport, practice against less skillful, unchallenging opponents may also lead to retention of a mediocre level of proficiency or performance deterioration. However, practicing against skilled players with the intent to improve is but one of the ingredients necessary for successfully developing a high level of skill proficiency; feedback is also essential. Without the help provided by appropriate, useful feedback, athletes are unguided in making their performance adjustments, may learn little that is necessary, or may even adopt incorrect technique. (You will learn more about feedback in chapter 8.)

This chapter concerns practice and, especially, the variables you must consider to make your practices more effective. Skills may be practiced in many different ways, under fatigued or nonfatigued conditions, for various

amounts of time, and according to different schedules. The question is how to manipulate these practice variables to meet the needs of your athletes. For example, would it improve your athletes' rate of learning and overall performance if they practiced 5 days a week instead of 3 days a week? How long should you allow your athletes to practice a new skill? In this chapter we will discuss these and many other practice variables. Our intent is to build on the practice principles that were introduced in *Coaching Young Athletes* (Martens et al., 1981) (summarized in chapter 1 of this book). The following specific topics are considered:

- Length and frequency of practice
- Effectiveness of massed and distributed practice
- Value of overpracticing skills
- Effects of practicing in a fatigued state
- Practicing for speed versus practicing for accuracy
- Role of errors in practicing a new skill
- Performance plateaus in practice

LENGTH AND FREQUENCY OF PRACTICE

How long and how often should your athletes practice skills to learn them well enough to achieve a consistent and high level of performance? To answer this question you need to be able to differentiate two factors: *within* practice session variables and *between* practice session variables.

In general, how you divide a practice session into periods of activity and rest is what we mean by *within* practice variables. For example, skills that are fatiguing can be practiced for only a short period of time before the athletes need time for rest and recovery. Skills requiring rapid movements, such as sprinting or skills that demand strenuous exertion, like wrestling, are especially exhausting and require frequent rest periods. Skills like those employed in soccer, on the other hand, often need to be practiced without any rest periods. Although soccer utilizes many rapid movements, players must often be able to perform after having already run several miles without any rest. As a general guideline, however, the National Association for Sport and Physical Education (Martens & Seefeldt, 1979) recommends that a single practice session last about 1 hour for children under 11 years of age and about 1½ hours for older athletes.

How you space successive practices is what we mean by *between* practice variables. For instance, your practices might be scheduled as often as three times a day if you are coaching swimming or the triathlon, or only once every week if you or your athletes cannot find the time for more frequent practices.

Within a Practice: When to Practice and When to Rest

Suppose you are coaching basketball. You want to teach your athletes the skill setting a pick (screen) and have allocated 30 minutes for this task. How should you divide the time? How will you determine the *practice distribution*?

When discussing practice distribution we often make a distinction between distributed and massed practice. Massed practice of a skill consists of continual practice with either no rest periods or brief and/or infrequent ones. Distributed practice of a skill consists of longer and/or more frequent rest periods between practice periods. As illustrated in Figure 6.1, these two types of practice lie at opposite ends of a continuum.

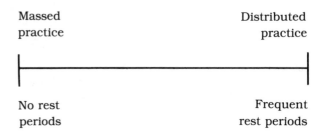

Figure 6.1   Massed and distributed practice lie on a continuum from having little or no rest to having longer, more frequent rest periods.

At one extreme, practice can be entirely massed; the skill is practiced until learned without taking any rest breaks. At the other extreme, practice can be divided into numerous periods of practice and rest, and breaks are permitted whenever desired. In this system rest may also refer to resting from one skill by practicing another. Between these two extremes exist the many different ways a coach can combine practice and rest periods to create an effective learning environment. For example, a few of the ways you could divide the basketball practice time are the following:

- Practice for 5 minutes, rest 1 minute, repeat 5 times.
- Practice for 10 minutes, rest 5 minutes, repeat 2 times.
- Practice continuously for 30 minutes.
- Practice for 5 minutes, perform other skills for 5 minutes, repeat 3 times.
- Practice for 4 minutes, rest 6 minutes, repeat 3 times.

Which is the most effective practice format? Unfortunately, there is no simple answer, although we will offer some guidelines. Each coach must discover the form of practice distribution that is most appropriate for the skills being learned and the athletes being taught. When making this decision, many factors ought to be considered: time of season, age of athletes, skill level of athletes, whether at the beginning of the practice or at the end, whether the sport requires repeated performances, and so forth. The point to remember is that different ratios of practice to rest will produce different results. We will discuss the advantages and disadvantages of the different forms of practice distribution in greater detail after we have examined the topic of practice frequency.

Practice Frequency

How often are you and your athletes willing and able to meet? The main training limitations for most coaches are time and other responsibilities. You and your athletes have other commitments in life, including school, family, and job. However, evidence shows that daily, twice daily, or even more frequent practice sessions will produce the greatest amount of learning. Once a skill has been well learned, less practice is required to maintain a particular level of skill. The physiological and psychological effects of high frequency practice place limits on the amount of practice that is beneficial to athletes. Some activities are much too strenuous for frequent practice sessions, and others are far too boring. Monitor closely how your athletes are reacting to the frequency and length of your practices and carefully consider your athletes' needs rather than simply following the traditions of your sport. We also recommend that you try to vary the drills, rotate your athletes to different work stations, and think of different ways to hold their interest.

One way in which physiological limitations can be overcome is to devise exercises and drills that use different muscle groups, thus avoiding the problems associated with fatigue. For example, if your athletes lifted weights with the legs one day and with the arms the next day, each muscle group would have 48 hours to recover, and fatigue would not be an issue of concern.

Some coaches believe that great athletes are born and not made, but research indicates a close relationship between skill level and number of practice hours. Young athletes who perform at exceptionally high levels usually do so because they have spent many hours in practice. Obviously, social and psychological factors must be considered, but from a skill-learning perspective, acquiring the highest levels of skill requires many practice hours. Estimates of practice time are illustrated in Table 6.1. Notice that it takes approximately 1 million repetitions—and sometimes more— to produce high-level performance in most skills.

Table 6.1
Estimates of repetitions of precise performance of a movement pattern to develop a motor program of skillful coordination *

Skill	Performer	Repetitions for skillful performance	Basis for estimate
Passing	Quarterback	1.4 million passes	15 yr × 200 days × 4 hr × 2/min
Punting	Football player	0.8 million	200/day × 5 days × 45 wk × 15 yr
Shooting	Basketball player	1 million baskets	Estimate of practice time
Pitching	Baseball pitcher	1.6 million throws	3/min × 180 min × 300 days × 10 yr
Gymnastics	14-year-old female gymnast	?	8 yr daily practice

*From ''The Training of Coordination'' by F. J. Kottke, D. Halpern, J. K. Easton, A. T. Ozel, and B. S. Burrill, 1978, *Archives of Physical Medicine and Rehabilitation*, **59**, p. 571. Copyright 1978 by the American Congress of Rehabilitation Medicine. Adapted by permission.

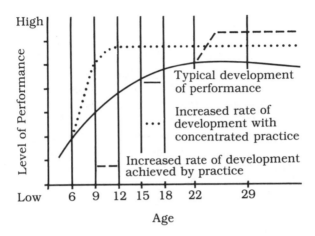

Figure 6.2 Concentrated practice can increase the rate of development of performance. From "The Training of Coordination" by F.J. Kottke, D. Halpern, J.K. Easton, A.T. Ozel, and B.S. Burrill, 1978, *Archives of Physical Medicine and Rehabilitation,* **59**, p. 569. Copyright 1978 by the American Congress of Rehabilitation Medicine. Adapted by permission.

Figure 6.2 shows how the rate of performance development can be increased in childhood and adulthood with concentrated practice. If you coach in a league whose season extends for several months, you'll understand how essential it is for your athletes to have developed their skills to a high level to begin the competitive season. Before league competition begins, you will have arranged practices as frequently as you can to teach the skills required. But as the season progresses, your athletes should need less and less practice to maintain their fitness and skill levels. Take care to avoid organizing too much practice later in the season or your players may lose their competitive edge, become bored, and drop out. Toward the end of the season, design your practices to keep your players sharp and ready for competition.

EFFECTIVENESS OF MASSED AND DISTRIBUTED PRACTICE

In the basketball coaching example previously introduced, we noted five alternatives for practice distribution in a 30-minute session, ranging from 30 minutes practicing continuously (massed practice, no rest periods) to a variety of combinations of practice distributions (various frequencies and durations of rest periods).

The following sections will discuss the relative merits of massed and distributed practice and will examine the relative effectiveness of the practice distributions suggested earlier in this chapter.

Massed Practice

Although the apparent advantage of massed practice is that athletes spend the maximum time practicing the skill, some coaches believe that a more distributed practice schedule is always more beneficial for learning a skill. The available research does not support this belief however, except when the massed practice induces severe fatigue in the athletes. Furthermore, if the fatigued athletes are given an adequate rest, their performance improves to approximately the level it would have been had they practiced under the distributed schedule. (Researchers refer to this dramatic improvement in performance after a period of rest and no practice as *reminiscence*.) Research indicates that performance tends to be poorer while the skill is being practiced under a massed schedule than it is when being practiced under a distributed schedule.

These findings suggest that a massed practice schedule that does not lead to severe fatigue temporarily depresses the performance of the skill but does not impair the final level of learning. Of course, the distinction between level of learning and level of performance, discussed in chapter 2, is quite important. Poor performance caused by fatigue is easily remedied with rest; poor performance resulting from failure to learn the skill adequately is something else entirely.

In any case, coaches utilizing a massed schedule, for example, to teach their players the pick in basketball (30 minutes continuously practicing, in our example) or to prepare their athletes for upcoming contests should be aware that it will adversely affect performance. However, they need not be too concerned about whether the massed practice of a skill will adversely affect learning.

Coaches should not, therefore, indiscriminately use massed and distributed schedules. Variables other than learning and performance create situations in which either distributed practice or massed practice is preferred.

Massed practice is the method of choice under the following conditions:

- The skill to be learned can be easily performed and quickly mastered.
- Motivation to continue to learn the skill is high.
- The purpose is to simulate the fatigued conditions an athlete might experience during a game or competition.
- Little time is available for your athletes to learn the skills needed to perform in the next game or competition.
- The athletes are in a later stage of learning, and their skill level and physical conditioning are very high.

Distributed Practice

Let us consider the effectiveness of the alternative practice schedules. The first schedule (practice for 5 minutes, rest 1 minute, repeat 5 times) may be best because it allow 25 minutes of actual practice time but still allows time for rest. If your athletes are relatively fit and experienced and need relatively little time to discuss what to do, this seems like a useful choice.

If you are coaching younger athletes, however, practicing for 5 minutes, performing other skills for 5 minutes, and repeating the cycle three times (the fourth schedule) is probably best because it gives the athletes a break from the intensity of practicing a new skill and the opportunity to practice other recently learned skills.

Distributed practice is preferred under the following conditions:

- Learning a new, complex skill.
- Learning a skill demanding so much mental and physical effort that fatigue can lead to injury—for example, attempting to perform twists and somersaults in gymnastics or diving when there is danger of fatigue.
- Fatigue is causing athletes to learn incorrect motor patterns.
- Attention span is short, such as when coaching very young athletes.
- Motivation to learn the skill is low.
- Athletes are not sufficiently conditioned for repetitive performance, such as in the early part of the season.
- The weather is hot and humid—exercise under these conditions can lead to dehydration and heat stress syndrome.

Duration, Intensity, and Frequency

Another way to determine the best practice design is to consider factors of duration, intensity, and frequency of practice. Different sports demand different levels of physiological conditioning, and these levels can be influenced by manipulating the duration, intensity, and frequency of practice. The requirements of each sport will often determine the nature of practice. At one end of the continuum of practice distribution is an activity like the sprint-start, which is probably best learned and performed using long rest intervals. You should use short periods of activity (duration) and maximal effort (intensity), and you should hold practice two or three times a week (frequency). In comparison, soccer skills are better learned with longer sessions, shorter rest periods, and more frequent practice sessions. Soccer players will improve faster if they practice seeing, kicking, and dribbling the ball thousands of times under a wide variety of physical and environmental conditions. These skills benefit from longer duration, lower intensity, and higher frequency activity periods.

If you coach sports that have high physical demands, such as running, swimming, cycling, skiing, or wrestling, sufficient rest periods should be interspersed in the practice schedule. Researchers have shown that a strategy of resting between intervals of strenuous exercise can reduce fatigue and increase the total volume of exercise that an athlete can perform in a workout.

VALUE OF OVERPRACTICING SKILLS

Overpractice occurs when athletes continue to practice after an acceptable performance criterion has been reached. In short, overpractice is practicing a skill that has already been learned. The more important the skill is to successful performance in the sport, the more coaches have their athletes overpractice it to ensure that they will be able to perform it effectively when needed in competition. The amount of overpractice used depends not only on the relative importance of the skill but on the quantity of practice time available and the level of anticipated benefit from the extra practice.

In the terms of our basketball example, you might be satisfied that your athletes have learned the free throw in basketball when they can consistently shoot 80%. If you consider the free throw to be very important, however, you may continue to have your athletes practice it so that they will be able to consistently maintain their 80% shooting average and perhaps even improve it. Moreover, overpractice benefits are likely to strengthen your athletes' confidence in their ability to perform the free throw successfully at this level.

However, you must be careful when deciding how much time your athletes need to spend overpracticing the free throw because overpracticing does not always have beneficial effects. In fact, excessive overpractice is detrimental if it causes boredom or loss of concentration that results in learning bad habits. Furthermore, the increased time spent on overpracticing does not always produce proportional increases in the athletes' ability to maintain their skill level consistently or to improve it. There is a point of diminishing returns—a point when additional time spent overpracticing a skill is wasted and would be more profitably spent practicing another skill. For example, you may decide to have your players spend 15 minutes overpracticing the free throw instead of 30 minutes because the additional shooting consistency is not worth the extra time and effort. You will use the remaining 15 minutes to have your players practice shooting lay-ups with the left hand because it is one of many important basketball skills that need to be perfected.

EFFECTS OF PRACTICING WHILE FATIGUED

Does practicing skills while fatigued have any significant effects on learning? This question is critical when deciding how to structure your practice session. In this discussion, *fatigue* refers both to specific muscle fatigue—the type your athletes experience in their arms and legs toward the end of a strenuous workout or competition—as well as to general tiredness.

Coaches often have to prepare their athletes for competition by having them practice skills in the same fatigued state they will experience during competition. The desired level of fatigue is usually induced by having them practice skills continuously (massed practice) or by scheduling very few rest intervals. Additionally, many coaches will have their athletes perform various physical exercises, such as running or calisthenics, before beginning to practice skills so that the athletes are fatigued as practice commences. The exercises may be alternated with skill practice to maintain or increase the level of fatigue as practice continues. Regardless of how the fatigued state is induced, however, the effect on performance should be no surprise: The greater the fatigue, the more skill performance suffers.

But what about skill learning? Does practicing a skill while fatigued have the same negative effect on learning that it does on performance? Perhaps fatigue is similar to the variables (discussed in chapter 2) that adversely affect performance but not learning. You may remember that we infer from performance whether or not learning has occurred. Based on the limited research available, light to moderate fatigue, and in some instances even moderately high fatigue, temporarily depresses skill *performance* with little or no damage to *learning*. However, severe fatigue has been shown to be detrimental to both performance and learning. This effect seems highly likely, especially if fatigue is so severe that it causes your athletes to practice movement patterns incorrectly. However, this effect occurs only when your athletes are extremely fatigued throughout the time they are practicing a new skill. If they are extremely fatigued before the practice of the skill begins but are allowed to recover while practicing the skill—you might allow more rest periods than normal—their learning is less likely to be affected adversely. On the other hand, if severe fatigue occurs immediately or shortly after the new skill has been practiced, their learning can be impaired.

In summary, practicing skills while moderately fatigued is unlikely to interfere with learning. Moreover, it is likely to improve the physical conditioning of athletes as well as their skill performance in the fatigued states that they will encounter in actual competitive situations. Nevertheless, practicing skills while severely fatigued is not recommended. Not only can excessive fatigue impair learning and performance, but it also risks the health of your athletes and increases their chances of injury.

PRACTICING FOR SPEED VERSUS PRACTICING FOR ACCURACY

One problem many coaches encounter when their athletes are learning a new skill is deciding whether to have them practice the skill at full speed, placing less emphasis on movement accuracy and form, or to have them practice the skill more slowly to emphasize movement accuracy. Some coaches believe that movement accuracy should be emphasized at the outset of learning; as practice continues, they reason, the speed of performing the skill can be gradually increased without sacrificing movement accuracy attained using the initially slower speed. If movement accuracy diminishes when speed is increased, they reinstitute a slower practicing speed to reestablish movement accuracy. This procedure is followed until both speed and accuracy are executed by the athletes at the proper level. This method obviously emphasizes accuracy of performance in the design of practice.

Other coaches, however, prefer a different approach. They believe that movement speed should be emphasized at the beginning of learning, so they have their athletes practice the skill at full speed, provided only that it can be executed safely and with a reasonable degree of movement accuracy. As practice continues, these coaches expect their athletes' movement accuracy to improve gradually and eventually to reach the level necessary for performing the skill successfully in competition.

There is yet another approach: coaches who emphasize movement accuracy and speed equally from the very beginning of learning. Their athletes gradually increase their movement speed and improve movement accuracy together until they can reach the speed and accuracy needed to perform the skill successfully in competition.

Which of these three practice approaches is the most beneficial for sport skill learning? In general, it is best to practice skills as they will have to be performed in competition as soon as possible, provided they can be performed safely and with a reasonable degree of movement accuracy. Skills demanding both movement accuracy and speed for successful performance in competition require you to emphasize both while practicing. However, when you are undecided about placing more emphasis on movement accuracy or speed, we recommend that you favor movement speed so that your athletes will learn the proper timing of the skill. Practicing a skill at competitive performance speed usually produces better results than extended practice at a slower speed emphasizing the accuracy of the movements. Care must be taken, of course, to ensure that your athletes can execute the skill at full speed safely and with a reasonable degree of movement accuracy, otherwise negative consequences may result. For example, would it be a more effective learning experience for a novice tennis player to swing at full speed and consistently miss the ball or to swing more slowly and hit the ball successfully? It would be difficult to convince the player of the rationale behind the emphasis on speed in the face of such obvious failure. Remember, in the absence of success, participation in sport rapidly loses its appeal. Before you emphasize speed, your athletes should be able to execute the skill with a reasonable degree of movement accuracy, safety, and success.

ROLE OF ERRORS IN PRACTICING A NEW SKILL

To what extent should you allow your athletes to make errors in practice when they are learning a skill? One view is that athletes should not experience errors in the course of learning a skill because errors lead to a lack of reinforcement and, it is thought, experiencing errors can only result in athletes becoming frustrated and discouraged. Furthermore, according to this view, the errors made in practice will become learned and repeated in the future in place of the correct response. Thus, practice conditions should be designed to eliminate or minimize the possibility of making errors while learning a skill. The learner should be physically directed through the correct movement pattern and prevented from making incorrect movements by utilizing manual guidance or appropriate apparatus.

However, the limited research evidence that exists on the role of errors suggests that such a practice is probably too extreme. The evidence indicates that experiencing errors while acquiring a skill is not harmful provided the athletes learn from their errors rather than learning the errors themselves. To ensure this outcome, practice conditions must be designed so that effective feedback is given to guide each athlete's performance, thus preventing errors from being repeated and internalized. Each athlete must be given corrective feedback about the error being made; once the athlete understands the feedback, he or she must have the opportunity to practice and learn to correct the error.

Letting athletes learn from their errors is advantageous. They are more likely to be able to correct these same errors if they occur again in future performances than athletes who were never given a chance to learn from their errors. In addition, when feedback is not available, they may be more effective in adjusting to errors they've never experienced before for two reasons: First, they are more experienced at the trial-and-error correction process than those who were not allowed to use this process; second, they have a more thorough understanding about how to perform the skill as a result of having experienced executing a wide range of variations of the skill instead of only the correct variation. Athletes who have more thorough understanding are more likely to be able to analyze incorrect performance of the skill and to generate new movements that will correct the errors.

In summary, you should not be overly concerned if your athletes make errors while attempting to learn a skill. Errors are a natural and important part of the learning process; your athletes can learn from them if given proper feedback. Designing artificial guidance conditions that prevent making errors and using them for an extended period of time in the course of learning a skill is not recommended. Instead we recommend that you allow your athletes to learn from their errors by conscientiously providing beneficial feedback and by designing appropriate practices.

PERFORMANCE PLATEAUS IN PRACTICE

Have you noticed that athletes and sometimes whole teams improve performance up to a certain level and then seem unable to improve with continued practice? This leveling off in performance is known as reaching a *performance plateau*. But why does it occur? Is it inevitable or avoidable? Before answering these questions consider what a *plateau* is. In some sports you can keep track of changes in your athletes performance by plotting a performance curve. Figure 6.3 shows a graph of the performance curve of a long jumper during a season.

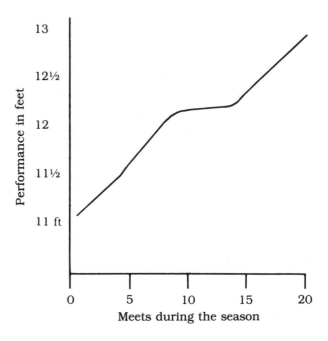

Figure 6.3 Performance plateau occurring during the course of the season.

You will notice that the athlete competed 20 times. At the start of the season performance improved; it then tapered off before picking up again toward the end of the season. The tapering off point is call a *plateau* because it looks flat when graphed.

Causes of Plateaus

Plateaus occur for four main reasons: (a) changes in cognitive strategy, (b) changes in technique, (c) psychological factors, and (d) physical fitness deficiencies. In all situations it is your job to be sure that your athletes understand what is happening and to help them cope with the changes that are occurring.

Changes in Cognitive Strategy

Plateaus can occur when individuals are in transition between cognitive strategies. Such strategies refer to the thoughts an athlete has before and during performance. In the example of the long jumper, the cause of the plateau could have been a decision to try different cognitive strategies in an effort to execute the skill more effectively. While trying these strategies, which were incorrect or no better than those used to learn the skill, performance did not improve but only leveled off. Once the appropriate strategy was found, improvement resumed.

Changes in Technique

Let's consider another example. A gymnast experiences a plateau because she has changed her skill technique. Her coach decided to increase the difficulty of her floor routine halfway through the season. Initially, she found it much harder to perform the new routine, and the added difficulty kept her from improving her performances. Eventually, however, she mastered the routine and her performance scores started to improve again.

Let's consider a performance plateau affecting the shot put. The skill is sometimes taught by omitting the glide at first. The athlete learns only to rotate and extend the arms. After these steps are mastered the glide is introduced, and as a result performance may level off or even deteriorate. However, as the glide becomes incorporated into shot put technique, performance should start to improve again. Another plateau may then be reached if the coach teaches the athlete to reverse his or her feet at the end of the shot put.

Plateaus can also occur in team performances as a result of changes in strategy. Learning a new strategy takes time. If a football team decides to change from emphasizing a running game to equally utilizing both running and throwing, its yardage may not increase. However, after a few games both running and passing may improve: The running game can gain more yards because of decreased pressure on it, and the throwing game can gain more yardage because of increased opportunities.

Psychological Factors

Why do plateaus occur? One explanation points to the existence of a skill-learning hierarchy: One set of skills must be learned before the next set can be initiated, like the construction of a building, beginning with the foundations then gradually moving upward brick by brick. Other reasons for plateaus are psychological and include anxiety, lack of motivation, boredom, and emotional problems. Regardless of the cause, however, your athletes are likely to experience a performance plateau related to psychological factors at one time or another. When this happens, what should you do? Fortunately, the typical situation resolves itself if you and your athletes have patience.

Remember, a plateau usually indicates a period of transition. By showing understanding and encouraging your athletes to be patient, you can help them through this transition. However, the ultimate key to supporting your athletes through a plateau period is to let them know that plateaus or performance decrements are natural parts of the learning process. Help them to understand rather than fear the performance plateau.

Physical Fitness Deficiencies

A fourth possible reason for a performance plateau is that your athletes have a deficiency in physical fitness under a specific training regimen. If you detect fitness deficiencies, evaluate your training program and identify the changes that can be made immediately and those that should be put off until the following season. For example, some athletes may lack the speed to perform very much beyond their current level; others may lack sufficient strength or muscular endurance. These limitations would be difficult to resolve in a short time period but could be taken into account in a new training program. For more information on designing a fitness program for your athletes, see the *Coaches Guide to Sport Physiology* (Sharkey, 1986).

Overcoming Plateaus

The suggestions presented in Table 6.2 identify some causes and possible solutions to performance plateaus.

Table 6.2
Causes and Remedies for Performance Plateaus*

Cause	Remedy
1. Loss of interest, loss of novelty, loss of motivation	Make practice appealing. Look for alternative approaches. Be enthusiastic, supportive, and encouraging. Use reinforcement.
2. Focus on wrong cues	Maintain the learner's attention to the appropriate cues so that practice is meaningful. Provide knowledge of results.
3. Fatigue	Be alert to situation. Stop practice or practice something else.
4. Emotions	Let learner progress slowly. Provide security.
5. Lack of physical readiness	Analyze the task demands and the learner's physical development. He or she may possess physical capacities to perform a task at a certain level of proficiency but will need further development if higher-order skills are to be demonstrated.
6. Setting low goals	Help the learner establish realistically high but attainable goals.
7. Lack of understanding of directions, lack of ability to recognize and adapt skills	Make a task analysis by subdividing the activity into smaller units so that transitions are smooth and logical from one performance level to a higher level of expectation. Allowing the learner to progress too fast in a complex activity places hardships on the ability to apply lower-order learned skills to higher-order ones and to comprehend and use instructions and directions effectively.

*From *Motor Learning and Human Performance* (pp. 39-40) by R.N. Singer, 1980, New York: Macmillan. Copyright 1980 by Robert N. Singer. Modified by permission.

SUMMARY AND RECOMMENDATIONS

In this chapter we discussed skill practice and some of the major factors influencing its effectiveness. The following list of guidelines summarizes what was presented and should be kept in mind as you plan and implement your practices.

1. Practice, alone, is insufficient for learning a skill correctly. To make practice effective you must (a) motivate your athletes to learn and (b) give them feedback about what they are doing correctly and incorrectly and about how their errors can be corrected.
2. Distribute practice during the early stage of learning complex skills and mass practice in the later stage.
3. Practice skills in the same way and under the same conditions required to perform in an actual competition as soon as your athletes are able to do so safely and accurately.
4. Practicing skills in a moderately fatigued state is likely to interfere with performance but has little or no effect on learning. However, practicing skills in a severely fatigued state, which is not

recommended, will be detrimental to both performance and learning.

5. Skills requiring equal emphasis on speed and accuracy for successful performance should be practiced by placing equal emphasis on both.

6. Although your athletes can improve or maintain their level of proficiency if given the opportunity to overpractice more important skills, care must be taken to ensure (a) that they are not becoming bored and learning bad habits and (b) that the time spent overpracticing is the best use of that time.

7. If performance plateaus occur, reevaluate your athletes' performance. Don't jump to conclusions. Analyze the situation thoroughly and gather all the facts available. If necessary, speak with your assistant coaches, athletes, and parents to help determine the cause of the plateau. Once the cause is determined, the solution (as suggested in Table 6.2) is usually apparent.

Chapter 7

Making Complex Skills Easier to Learn

One of the most challenging tasks you will face is introducing new and often quite complex skills to your athletes. You can make *complex* skills easier to learn if you have your athletes practice the parts of the skill before they try the whole skill. By dividing skills into parts, you can help your athletes avoid many of the difficulties novices experience when they attempt to perform a movement that is just too complex. For example, imagine trying to teach a beginning athlete how to dribble an ice hockey puck the length of the rink and score a goal. What would happen if you demonstrated the skill and then asked the athlete to imitate you? It would probably be a disaster, especially if the athlete could not skate. Some skills are simply too complex to learn without being broken down into smaller components and mastering the components in a logical order. Very few skills can initially be taught exactly as they are to be performed in competitive situations. To become an effective coach you need to develop the ability to break skills down into parts your athletes can easily learn and then help recombine the parts into the whole skill.

Another way you can make complex new skills or knowledge easier to learn is to have your athletes make use of their previously acquired skills and knowledge. In this chapter we will discuss two major topics:

- Whole and part methods of teaching
- Teaching for positive transfer between skills

How would one teach stickhandling and shooting? An ice hockey coach would almost certainly first teach an athlete basic skating skills and make sure the athlete knew how to hold the stick to control the puck from a stationary position. Stickhandling and shooting instruction would then follow, until finally the athlete would be able to combine the skating and hockey skills to perform the desired stickhandling and shooting drill. Let's look at this process of breaking skills down for instruction in more detail.

WHOLE AND PART METHODS OF TEACHING

In the purest sense, the *whole* method of teaching requires that athletes learn the activity or skill as a single unit. At the other end of the continuum is the *part* method, which requires that your athletes learn each component of the whole activity before attempting to integrate the parts to form the whole activity. Throughout the season you will find yourself using a combination of these two methods in an attempt to take advantage of the special strengths of your athletes in various learning situations.

Before examining whole and part methods of teaching in more detail, you need to know what we mean by a whole and a part. We could define the whole as an entire game (e.g., soccer). If we do so, the parts would be the fundamental skills of the game (e.g., dribbling, kicking, heading, trapping), combinations of these skills, and offensive and defensive plays.

On the other hand, we could take a more restricted view of the whole and define it as any one of the fundamental skills of a sport, such as a forehand stroke in tennis, a lay-up shot in basketball, or a sacrifice bunt in baseball. In this case a part would be a component of the whole skill that could be isolated and practiced on its own. For instance, in the tennis forehand stroke—the whole skill—we could arbitrarily identify the parts of grip, footwork, backswing, forward stroke, and follow-through. As you can see, defining a whole is up to you as long as it is independent and has meaning in itself beyond that implied by its parts. Furthermore, what constitutes a part depends on how you define the whole because a part is a component of the whole that is necessary to the meaning of the whole but that loses its special meaning when separated from the whole.

Let us now consider different ways of teaching a skill like the basketball lay-up shot if that skill is defined as the whole. Most coaches would realize that this skill is too complicated to learn without breaking it down into small components. One way to begin teaching it is to identify the following three components: (a) dribbling the basketball close to the basket (dribbling), (b) coordinating opposite limbs because the takeoff and the shot are performed with the opposite arm and leg (takeoff), and (c) controlling the basketball with the shooting hand (shooting). These components could be taught in a variety of ways, and six possible methods are listed. As you consider each method, analyze how it could be used to teach the skills in the sport that you coach.

- Part-whole method
- Progressive-part method
- Repetitive-part method
- Whole-part-whole method
- Whole method
- Backward chaining method

Part-Whole Method

This method involves teaching the parts one after the other and having your athletes learn each of them before they attempt the whole. For example, one sequence for teaching the lay-up skill would be (a) teach how to dribble the basketball, (b) then teach the takeoff, (c) then teach how to shoot, and, finally, (d) teach the lay-up as a whole once each of the three parts has been mastered. We do not recommend that you use this method to teach skills like the lay-up because the parts form a sequence of actions that need to be practiced together. The part-whole method is more useful when the parts do not seem to form a natural and meaningful sequence of actions and therefore do not need to be practiced together. When the game of basketball is defined as the whole, examples of nonsequential parts can be found, such as (a) the technique used to execute a foul shot, (b) guarding an opponent using man-to-man defense, and (c) maneuvering to get possession on a jump ball. No apparent purpose is served by practicing these parts in sequential combination, and parts of this variety are best practiced using the part-whole method. They can be learned in any order, practiced separately, and, once mastered, can be incorporated into the game.

Progressive-Part Method

When this method is used you teach one part, then another. When the two parts are mastered, they are combined and practiced together until learned. Then the third part is taught by itself. After it is acquired the three parts are combined and practiced together until learned. This procedure is followed for each of the remaining parts until all of them can be practiced as a whole. The progressive-part method is appropriate to use when the parts form a natural and meaningful sequence of actions and thus need to be practiced together.

If you were using this method to teach the lay-up shot, you would (a) teach how to dribble the basketball and practice until it is mastered; (b) teach the takeoff; (c) combine dribbling and takeoff, practicing them together until they are mastered; (d) teach how to shoot, practicing until it is mastered; and (e) combine dribbling, takeoff, and shooting, practicing them together as a whole until the whole skill is mastered.

Repetitive-Part Method

The repetitive-part method involves teaching and practicing a part until it is learned, and then combining it with a new part and teaching and practicing them together until they are learned. These two parts are then combined with a third part and taught and practiced together until they are mastered. This procedure is followed for each of the remaining parts until all of the parts can be practiced as a whole. The repetitive-part method is a variation of the progressive-part method and would be used in similar situations.

If you were using this method to teach the lay-up shot, you would (a) teach how to dribble the basketball, practicing it until it is mastered; (b) combine dribbling with takeoff, teaching and practicing them together until they are acquired; and (c) combine dribbling, takeoff, and shooting and teach and practice them together as a whole.

Whole-Part-Whole Method

This method involves first teaching and practicing the whole and then teaching and practicing one of its parts. Once the part is learned, the whole is practiced again. This procedure is repeated for each of the remaining parts. One way to employ this method to teach the lay-up shot would be to use the following sequence: (a) teach the lay-up shot and have your athletes practice it; (b) teach how to dribble, practicing it until it is learned; (c) practice the lay-up shot; (d) teach the takeoff, practicing it until it is acquired; (e) practice the lay-up shot; (f) teach how to shoot, practicing it until it is mastered; (g) practice the lay-up shot.

If you decide to adopt the whole-part-whole approach, you should arrange a good demonstration of the skill and have your athletes try to perform the whole skill. Careful observation of their performance will then enable you to decide which parts to teach and in what order.

After observing the performance of the whole skill long enough to decide which parts need the most practice, you should first demonstrate the most important part of the skill needing work. For example, the first thing a golf instructor might teach after the obser-

vation is how to grip the club because the grip is very important to how successfully a player makes contact with the ball.

If necessary, explain to your athletes how the parts to be practiced fit into the skill as a whole and why you are teaching the skills in a certain sequence. It may well be that some golfers respond better to different sequences; thus, careful observation of the initial whole performance is very important. If, for example, the golfer has a natural swing but a faulty grip, the coach would obviously concentrate on improving the grip. The athletes would practice assuming the correct grip, and as soon as they have shown improvement, the coach would have them practice the whole skill again. This procedure would continue until the athletes had learned the skill.

Whole Method

The whole method involves teaching and practicing the whole activity until it is learned. For the example of the lay-up you would teach the whole lay-up shot and have your athletes practice it until it is mastered.

The whole method is used most often for simple skills or for skills that are impossible to break down into component parts. Discrete tasks (those that have a definite beginning and end) of short duration, such as a soccer kick, are best suited for the whole method of instruction.

The swimming start is another skill that is usually learned through the whole method of instruction. A swimming coach would break down the key points of the racing start in the explanation and demonstration (e.g., foot placement, arm and leg position, and amount of arm swing). However, because the start is one rapid movement, it should be learned as such.

Backward Chaining Method

Backward chaining is a variation of the part teaching method. It is quite possible, and sometimes useful, to reverse the sequence in which, for example, the lay-up shot is learned. Your athletes could learn the shot before they learn take-off and the dribble. The main advantage of this approach is tht it can be more motivating to athletes because they get to perform the fun part, scoring a basket, first.

A similar approach has been adopted to teach golf: All shots are considered an extension of the putt, and all the other shots are made by extensions of the swing used in the putt. Thus golf can be taught by starting with the short putt and gradually introducing longer putts, chips, pitches, and drives as each

skill is mastered. A complete golf chain is shown in Table 7.1.

How might this approach be appropriate for teaching some of the skills in your sport?

Selecting the Best Method

There are no hard-and-fast rules to tell you which method to use for every situation. Some coaches are better at using one method than another and will tend to use it more often. Some athletes learn more effectively with one

Table 7.1
Complete Golf Chain and Mastery Criterion*

Step	Shot	Mastery Criterion
1	10-inch putt (between clubs optional)	four putts consecutively holed
2	16-inch putt	four putts consecutively holed
3	(between clubs optional)	
4	2-foot putt clubs removed	four putts consecutively holed
5	3-foot putt	four putts consecutively holed
6	4-foot putt, some break	two holed, two out of four with 6 inches
7	6-foot putt	four consecutively within 6 inches
8	10-foot putt	four consecutively within 12 inches
9	15-foot putt	four consecutively within 15 inches
10	20-foot putt	four consecutively within 18 inches
11	30-foot putt	four consecutively within 24 inches
12	35-foot chip 5 feet off green, 7-iron	four out of six within 6 feet
13	35-foot chip 15 feet off green, wedge	four out of six within 6 feet
14	65-foot chip	four out of six within 6 feet
15	25-yard pitch	four out of six within 10 feet
16	35-yard pitch	four out of six within 15 feet
17	50-yard pitch	four out of six within 15 feet
18	75-yard shot	four out of six within 30 feet
19	100-yard shot	four out of six within 40 feet
20	125-yard shot	four out of six within 45 feet
21	150-yard shot	four out of six within 54 feet
22	175-yard shot	four out of six within 66 feet
	200-yard shot (if within your range)	four out of six within 90 feet

*From *Total Golf: A Behavioral Approach to Lowering Your Score and Getting More Out of Your Game* by T.C. Simek and R.M. O'Brien, 1981, Huntington, NY: B-Mod Associates. Copyright 1981 by Thomas C. Simek and Richard M. O'Brien. Reprinted by permission.

method whereas others do better with another. Selecting the best method for your situation is not an easy task because so many factors must be considered.

When deciding whether to use the whole or part methods when teaching sport skills to your athletes, ask yourself the following key questions:

1. Can I teach the skill as a whole, or is it too complicated?

2. What is the best way to break down the skill into its parts and then help the athletes learn the parts well enough to be joined together and learned as a whole?

Generally, teaching a new skill as a whole is best if your athletes can perform it correctly and safely. When you have to utilize one of the part methods to teach a new skill, we strongly recommend that you always begin by introducing your athletes to how the whole skill should be performed and then relating the parts to the whole. Start with a demonstration of the whole skill that shows your athletes how the parts fit into the whole. After the demonstration, the skill can be broken down in a way that will help your athletes learn it with the least amount of difficulty.

Part methods of instruction are of greatest value when a skill is complex or involves separate, independently performed parts. For example, all of the swimming strokes are suited to part methods of instruction because the arms, legs, and breathing actions can be practiced independently. When using the part method, however, it is essential to appreciate that successful integration of the separate parts into the whole skill is likely to occur only if the parts can be performed as required when performing the whole skill. In the case of swimming, it is essential that the parts be linked together as soon as possible so that the athlete can learn the correct timing of the stroke. Remember, parts of a skill must be practiced in relation to the whole skill.

In summary, greater emphasis should be placed on the whole (a) if it can be understood in a meaningful way; (b) if it can be practiced safely and with a reasonable degree of success; (c) if the athletes are above-average learners, highly motivated, and have an extensive background of experience in various sports and skills; and (d) if the athletes have a long enough attention span to deal with the whole. When the opposite conditions prevail or when certain parts of the whole are being performed poorly and are in need of special attention, give more emphasis to part methods.

TEACHING FOR POSITIVE TRANSFER BETWEEN SKILLS

New and complex skills can often be made easier to learn if a coach teaches for positive transfer. *Transfer of learning* refers to the impact learning one skill can have on the subsequent learning of a different skill. Transfer may be positive, negative, or zero. When the learning of one skill facilitates the learning of another skill, *positive transfer* is occurring. For example, learning how to throw a baseball overhand can facilitate the learning of either a tennis serve or an overhand volleyball serve. The overhand throwing motion is quite similar between the skills and transfers positively. Learning how to kick a soccer ball can facilitate learning how to kick extra points and field goals in football. The soccer style of kicking transfers positively.

If learning one skill interferes with learning another, we refer to this as *negative transfer*. For example, learning various tennis strokes can interfere with learning certain badminton or racquetball strokes. Although the stroke patterns and eye-hand coordination are likely to transfer positively between skills, the rather rigid wrist action of tennis strokes is likely to interfere with learning the somewhat flexible wrist action used to execute badminton and racquetball strokes.

Finally, when learning a skill appears to have no influence on learning another skill, we say that *zero transfer* has occurred. For instance, learning how to shoot an arrow in target archery is unlikely to influence learning how to punt a football. Obviously, when teaching sport skills we would prefer for positive transfer to occur. The following sections will help you identify conditions that can increase the likelihood of positive transfer taking place.

Determine the Similarities Between Previously Learned Skills and the Skill About To Be Learned

The greater the similarity between two skills, the greater the possibility of positive transfer between them. This relationship is illustrated in Figure 7.1. For example, we might expect some positive transfer between a tennis serve and volleyball serve because of similarities in stimulus (a tossed ball) and response (an overhand throwing motion) requirements. Similarly, athletes who have had some prior exposure to gymnastics will probably learn diving skills faster because of similarities in the types of movement skills required.

Although you may expect similar skills to transfer positively, do not be surprised if some negative transfer is evident during the early learning stages. The evolution of the butterfly stroke in swimming illustrates how transfer may have an unpredictable initial effect. Prior to the 1960s butterfly swimmers used a breaststroke kick. When the dolphin kick was first introduced many swimmers found it difficult to synchronize the traditional arm action with the new leg kick. It took some time before swimmers learned to coordinate the stroke and to appreciate that the new technique was indeed faster than the old method.

When there is little or no connection between the stimulus and response requirements of two skills, little or no transfer should be expected. For example, zero transfer would be likely to occur if an athlete is learning both how to play golf and how to bowl. Moreover, the greatest learning difficulties seem to appear when two skills have opposite stimulus-response requirements, as in the butterfly stroke example just presented. The stimulus conditions (i.e., swimming conditions) were the same for performing the butterfly with either the breaststroke kick or the dolphin kick. In fact, part of the response requirements, the arm stroke, was the same for both

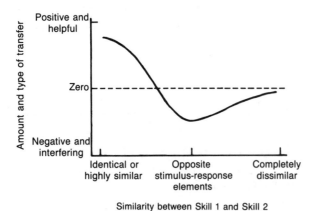

Figure 7.1 Effects of skill similarity on transfer of learning.

types of kicks, which allowed a degree of positive transfer. However, one aspect of the response requirements, the leg kick, was not the same, and this caused negative transfer to result between having learned to coordinate the traditional arm action with the breaststroke kick and learning to coordinate the traditional arm action with the new dolphin kick. The stimulus conditions were the same, but the response requirements had changed.

Explain the Similarities Between Skills

Coaches are strongly urged to point out the relationships between skills that are similar because the similarities may not be obvious to the athletes. Pointing out the relationships may increase the positive transfer of previously learned skills to the learning the new skill. From the outset your athletes should recognize the parts of the skills you hope will transfer and the parts that must not be transferred.

For example, let's suppose an athlete is trying to learn the tennis serve for the first time and is having difficulty moving the arm holding the racquet through the proper movement sequence. The athlete will probably find it helpful if you explain and demonstrate that service movements are similar to or different from a skill the athlete may already know—the overhand throw.

Explaining similarities and differences to enhance positive transfer is not limited to learning skills. Transfer is also an effective teaching technique when athletes are learning new strategies, concepts, or plays. When, for example, a basketball team is being taught the give-and-go or pass-and-cut for the first time, the skill may be learned faster if the coach points out how similar this play is to the give-and-go the athletes have already learned in soccer.

Similarly, in team sports many of the basic playing principles and strategies are identical. Effective coaches routinely integrate past and present learning experiences into their explanations and demonstrations. Remember, if you want positive transfer to occur, *teach* for it. Do *not* leave it to chance.

Explain the Mechanical Principles Common to Both Old and New Skills

Understanding the mechanical principles, strategies, and relationships between two skills has been shown to produce positive transfer. The classic study in this area (Judd, 1908) showed that a knowledge of the principle of light refraction improved the accuracy of subjects throwing darts at submerged targets. Nowadays, an explanation of Newton's laws of motion, presented at the appropriate level, may significantly improve the learning of swimmers, divers, gymnasts, figure skaters, and most other athletes attempting to learn new movement skills. But remember that it is not sufficient merely to expose the learner to the correct principles. Unless the learner understands and appreciates the significance of the information, it is unlikely he or she will be able to apply the knowledge in practice. You should take every opportunity to give your athletes practical, meaningful examples of the impact of mechanical principles on sport performance.

Be Sure That the Skills You Refer to Have Been Well Learned

The better the original skill has been learned, the more efficient its transfer to a subsequent skill. Therefore, if you want one skill you are teaching to transfer to another, you must be sure to provide adequate practice of the original skill. Inadequate practice and the resulting impaired learning will result in little or no positive transfer.

Be Sure That Skills Have Been Learned With the Dominant (Preferred) Limb Before Attempting to Transfer Learning to the Nondominant Limb

Bilateral transfer is the transfer from a limb on one side of the body to a limb on the opposite side. The greatest amount of bilateral transfer occurs in the identical muscle group on the side of the body opposite from the dominant limb.

Physiologists have found that the training of one limb muscle group can result in a strength gain in the same muscle group in the opposite limb. Research reviewed by Fischman, Christina, and Vercruyssen (1982) also suggests that bilateral transfer occurs in motor skill learning and that it occurs from hand to foot as well as hand to hand.

Sport settings present many potential applications for bilateral transfer of skill. In sports requiring ambidextrous use of the limbs, such as basketball, wrestling, handball, soccer, and volley ball, extensive practice with one limb may facilitate the rate of skill acquisition of the other limb when that limb is made to practice. As an example, if you want to develop a switch-hitter in baseball, you should be sure that the athlete is well into the intermediate stage of learning hitting with the preferred hand before suggesting that he or she hit from the other side. By following this procedure the initial learning would be more efficient, and the transfer to the nondominant limb would be more effective. Moreover, under conditions of fatigue or injury to the dominant limb, practice may continue with the other limb, which facilitates performance with the resting dominant limb.

Bilateral practice should not be introduced into your coaching sessions until your athletes have developed a reasonable degree of proficiency with the preferred limb. Once the learner has progressed past the beginning stage of learning and is well into the intermediate stage, practice with the nonpreferred limb can be incorporated into practice sessions.

Practice the Skill Under Competitive Conditions as Soon as Your Athletes Are Safely Able to Do So

Most coaches are able to make skills more difficult or easier by the control they exert over practice conditions. For example, some baseball coaches will decrease the size of the strike zone during practice in the hope that their pitchers will be more accurate when they return to the strike zone used in game condi-

tions. Other baseball coaches vary the difficulty of skills by changing the speed of the ball. They pitch at slow speeds to young players first learning to hit, hoping that learning to hit at slow speeds will transfer to learning to hit at fast speeds. Although these techniques may be effective for learning skills, the extent to which the experience will transfer to performance is limited. Practicing skills in this way is usually not as effective as practicing the skill as it will have to be performed in game conditions. Maximum transfer occurs when skills are practiced under conditions similar to those present during competition.

SUMMARY AND RECOMMENDATIONS

Some skills involve too many difficult movements to be learned all at once. They have to be divided into managable parts that athletes can learn. Consider the following points when breaking down skills:

1. Always begin with a demonstration of the whole skill.
2. Have your athletes initially attempt as much of a skill as is safe.
3. Each component of the skill should be capable of being performed as a skill in its own right.
4. Make sure that the parts can be easily integrated into the whole skill.
5. Consider using reverse chaining to teach skills in which each movement is an extension of the previous movement, as in the basketball lay-up shot.
6. Some skills can be made easier to learn by teaching for positive transfer. Follow these guidelines:

   - Determine the similarities between previously learned skills and the skill about to be learned.
   - Explain the similarities between skills to your athletes.
   - Explain the principles common to both the old and new skill.
   - Be sure the original skill has been well learned.

- Maximize transfer between limbs by overlearning the skill with the dominant limb first.

- Practice the skill under competitive conditions as soon as your athletes are safely able to do so.

Chapter 8
Feedback: Its Functions and Use in Teaching Skills

Imagine trying to putt a golf ball or shoot a foul shot in basketball wearing a blindfold with no one around to give you any advice. You probably would not do very well. Many young athletes feel very much the same way when learning skills because they are seldom explicitly told what to do or whether they performed the skill correctly. Even though they can see, they are often not told what to look at, what to look for, or what their performance looked like. To be an effective coach you need to develop the ability to teach sport skills in such a way that your athletes learn the skills correctly, with a minimum of frustration. A systematic approach is vital. Such an approach lets your athletes know how they are executing their skills and includes information about both the correct and the incorrect aspects of their performance. The information they receive about their performance is called *feedback*. Without feedback, systematic learning is impossible. In this chapter the following topics will be considered:

- Types and functions of feedback
- Feedback as information to correct errors
- Feedback as reinforcement to strengthen correct performance
- Feedback as punishment to eliminate errors
- Feedback as motivation for skill learning
- Using augmented feedback as positive reinforcement for skill shaping
- Using augmented feedback for skill modification

TYPES AND FUNCTIONS OF FEEDBACK

Two major types of feedback are available to athletes: intrinsic and augmented. *Intrinsic feedback* is the information athletes receive as a natural consequence of their performance. For instance, when players kick a soccer ball, kinesthetic feedback arising from sensory receptors located in their muscles, tendons, and joints provides them with knowledge about their kicking movement. Auditory feedback received through players' ears enable them to hear the sounds associated with the kick itself. Touch and pressure receptors allow them to feel the ground beneath their feet and the impact of the instep of their foot contacting the ball. After the ball is kicked and on its way, visual feedback received through their eyes allows them to see the flight of the ball and provides knowledge about how far and how accurately the ball has traveled.

Augmented feedback is information the athletes would not ordinarily receive as a natural consequence of their performance. It is provided by a source external to the athletes, such as a coach, teammate, mirror, or videotape system. Augmented feedback may be given verbally, as when a coach explains how to correct a performance error, or it may be presented nonverbally, as when a coach demonstrates how to correct an error or shows a videotape replay of an athlete's performance.

Whether it is intrinsic or augmented, feedback can serve four functions: *information or knowledge*, *reinforcement*, *punishment*, and *motivation*. Feedback that primarily acts as information or knowledge carries a message about the overall effectiveness of a skill performance, the errors that were made, and how to correct them. Feedback that reinforces a response strengthens that response, thereby increasing the likelihood that the response will be repeated in the future under similar conditions. In contrast, feedback that is perceived as punishment acts to suppress an undesirable response. Feedback that functions to motivate your athletes can arouse them to direct their effort to strive to improve their performance. These different functions are illustrated in Figure 8.1.

The following example of using feedback will give you a better appreciation of its four functions. With only 53 seconds left in the last game of the season, Coach Kathy Smith's team was down by 1 point with two time-outs left. She called time and set up a play the team had practiced all week. She carefully reminded her players what to do, and they executed the play perfectly. However, the opposition immediately came back down the court and scored. Kathy called her last time-out and said:

OK, we still have time left to win. The last play was great and just what I wanted [positive reinforcement]. We will use the same play again, but this time Joy will take the shot. After the shot make sure we get back and cover the break. Susan, stay much closer to the basket and don't get drawn out as you were last time [error correction information]. Barbara, stop taking cheap shots at your opponent; I've warned you about it before, and I want it stopped here and now [punishment]. All of you have worked hard all game and all season—let's give it one final effort [motivation]!

Kathy's players went back on the court, repeated the same offensive play, scored, then successfully defended for the remaining seconds to win the final game by a single point.

The following four sections describe each function of feedback in more detail. Consider how you might take advantage of the four functions of feedback in your sport situation.

FEEDBACK AS INFORMATION TO CORRECT ERRORS

Feedback that functions as information or knowledge to correct performance errors usually carries a message to the athlete about

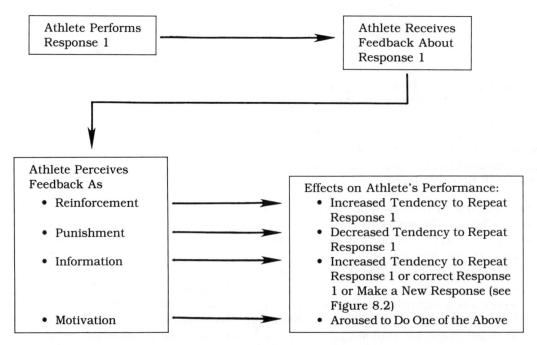

Figure 8.1 How feedback functions to influence an athlete's performance.

- the outcome of the performance (knowledge of results),
- the movement-produced sensations that accompany the performance (kinesthetic feedback),
- identifying the parts of the skill that were performed correctly and incorrectly (knowledge of performance),
- the explanation of the cause(s) of the error(s),
- changes in technique that must be made to correct the error(s), and
- the reasons why these particular changes were recommended.

How Information Feedback Works

The diagram in Figure 8.2 is a simplified model of the system by which an athlete uses information feedback to evaluate whether he or she responded correctly and, if not, what corrections need to be made. Figure 8.2 represents our old friend the motor program. You may recall from chapter 2 that a motor program is like a computer program for the brain that contains instructions for the execution of a response. When an athlete is going to make a response, the motor program tells the muscular system which muscles are to contract and how they are to contract to generate the desired response. Simultaneously, a copy of the commands sent to the muscular system is stored in the brain for response evaluation.

As the muscles contract and the response is being produced, sensory receptors in the muscles, tendons, and joints provide kinesthetic feedback through the athletes' sensory system for response evaluation. The athlete's brain uses a copy of the commands and kinesthetic feedback to evaluate whether or not the movement was correct and performed as intended. Regardless of the actual outcome of the response, if the response was performed as intended, the athlete experiences a feeling that it was correct; if the response was not executed as planned, the athlete experiences a feeling that it was incorrect. The more skilled the athlete, the greater the accuracy of the response evaluation. The response evaluation of athletes who are in the beginning stages of learning new sport skills is less accurate because they have not yet developed a memory for how the skill should feel when performed correctly.

In addition to kinesthetic feedback, your

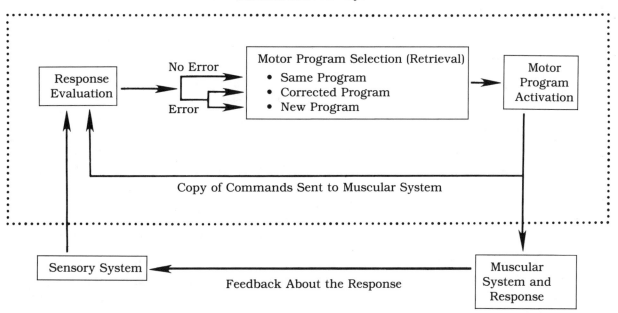

Central Nervous System

Figure 8.2 Simplified model of an athlete's system for using information feedback to evaluate the correctness of a response and make corrections.

athletes will also receive feedback about the response from other sensory receptors, such as their eyes (visual feedback) and ears (auditory feedback), and from external sources, such as coaches, teammates, spectators, and opponents. For example, if a basketball player misses a shot during practice, the movement response will usually feel wrong, and the player will see the ball miss the basket and perhaps even hear it hit the rim of the basket; the player might also receive feedback from the coach or teammates. All of these sources of feedback enter through the athlete's sensory system and travel to the brain, where the information is used to evaluate the correctness of the response that was just performed. If no error was detected, the athlete simply selects the same motor program again when the response is to be repeated. If an error was detected, however, the next time the movement is to be repeated the athlete selects either a corrected motor program or a new one.

Delivering Augmented Information Feedback

Your feedback should tell your athletes something more about their performance than their intrinsic feedback has already told them. Before you provide feedback always ask yourself the following questions: Am I giving my athletes information they don't already know about? Will this information help them maintain or improve their performance? Your feedback should provide specific information to correct errors and to reinforce correct technique.

As an example, consider the reaction of Sam, a coach who was clearly dissatisfied with the performance of his basketball players. Having watched two of his players practice the bounce pass and having seen that the ball was not getting high enough off the ground to be caught, he walked over to his players and said, "You just aren't doing it right, you're not trying hard enough!" Sam did provide his athletes with feedback because they now know that they are not performing the skill correctly, but how useful or effective was his advice? Instead of berating his players for lack of effort, Sam might have said: "John, you are

passing the ball too hard. Try to let the ball hit the court about two-thirds of the way towards Steve." These comments provide specific information about parts of the skill that were executed incorrectly, as well as instructions about how to correct them. Instead, Sam chose to offer comments high in judgment ("You aren't trying hard enough!") but low in information (trying harder will probably not correct John's error). Such comments not only have little or no impact on learning but they frequently dampen an athlete's enthusiasm for sport. This type of comment is worse than not commenting at all, and yet think how often you hear coaches yelling statements like "Try harder" or "You're still not doing it right" or "When are you going to get it right?" These comments serve little purpose except to frustrate the athletes, destroy their self-confidence, and erode the credibility of the coach.

A different example is illustrated by Coach Kathy Smith, who has just watched two groups of athletes perform a three-on-two basketball drill finishing with a shot at the basket. She wanted them to score on at least 8 of 10 attempts. They were successful, even though they failed on 2 attempts. Before proceeding to the next drill, Kathy complimented her athletes on accomplishing the task, giving them the following specific information on their performance: "The passes you were making behind the defender were excellent because they did not let her get back to cut off the shooter from the basket." Notice how this feedback carries information about the parts of the skill that were performed correctly; correct performance should be reinforced. However, Kathy's approach did not ignore the errors. After noting the parts of the drill the athletes performed correctly, she spent several minutes working on what had gone wrong on the two missed baskets. This approach increased her athletes' confidence but also showed them how they could become even better. When coaching your athletes, always try to identify the *cause* of their problems and look for solutions rather than judgments or criticisms.

How Often Should You Give Augmented Information Feedback?

Using augmented feedback as information (knowledge) to correct skill errors should follow a certain schedule. In the beginning stage of learning, give augmented information feedback each time the athlete performs the skill or as frequently as possible. Giving information feedback as often as possible early in learning is important because it will guide the athlete toward performing the skill correctly in less time than if feedback were given infrequently. It also increases the likelihood that the skill will more closely approximate the correct form at the outset of learning than if feedback were given less often. As learning progresses and performance of the skill improves, however, the augmented feedback you give should gradually become less and less frequent so that the athlete gradually learns to become less and less dependent on it to perform the skill successfully. Upon reaching the advanced stage of learning, the athlete needs to receive augmented information feedback only occasionally to be certain he or she is performing the skill correctly.

In situations in which you have a large number of athletes on your team and too few assistant coaches to give feedback as often as it should be given early in learning, you can have your athletes, if they are able, give feedback to each other. For example, to practice trapping skills in soccer you could arrange your athletes in groups of three. One athlete performs the trapping skills, another throws the ball to be trapped, and the third gives the

feedback. After a certain time period or number of attempts to perform the skill, the players would change positions until each has experienced all three roles.

A word of caution, however: If youngsters are going to be used to give feedback, they must be told exactly what to look for when their teammates are performing the skill. They must also be told what the corrections are for common errors.

FEEDBACK AS REINFORCEMENT TO STRENGTHEN CORRECT PERFORMANCE

In addition to providing information about performance to correct errors, feedback also can function as *reinforcement*. When it serves as reinforcement feedback strengthens the response you want the athlete to learn, regardless of whether it is acting as positive or negative reinforcement.

Feedback as Positive Reinforcement

Feedback that acts as positive reinforcement has pleasant properties that an athlete will pursue if at all possible. However, for it to serve as positive reinforcement it must follow the response, preferably immediately, and increase the likelihood that the response will occur in the future under the same or similar conditions. Figure 8.3 illustrates how feedback functions as positive reinforcement.

An example of intrinsic feedback that may serve as positive reinforcement is the satisfaction of seeing the soccer ball you kicked go exactly where you planned it to go and sensing (via kinesthetic feedback) that your body moved precisely as you intended it to move when executing the kick. Intrinsic feedback consisting of this type of information can be quite rewarding, and to experience it again you will try to execute the kick in the same way in the future under similar conditions.

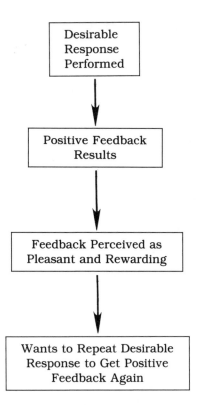

Figure 8.3 The desired response is strengthened when positive feedback occurs as a consequence of its performance.

Examples of augmented feedback that may act as positive reinforcement are verbal compliments or praise from a coach, like "Good try," "Great move" or "Your form was perfect, keep up the good work," and nonverbal types of communication, such as a smile or nod of approval or pat on the back. Receiving this kind of augmented feedback soon after you have successfully performed a skill can be very rewarding. To obtain it again you will try to perform the skill in the same way in the future under similar conditions. Some coaches believe that if they use augmented feedback as a reward for some action, it always will function as positive reinforcement. However, this is true only if the action is strengthened (if the chance that the action will occur in the future is increased), and that depends on whether the athlete, not the coach, perceives the augmented feedback as being a reward. What appears to be positive reinforcement to one person can be seen entirely differently by another. For example, changing an athlete's playing position

may be viewed by a coach as evidence of the athlete's all-around ability, but the athlete may be upset with the move because he or she sees it as a failure to play the first position well.

Regardless of how the athlete perceives the coach's reinforcement, he or she may still be unable to reproduce the original skilled performance. As we will see in part 4, the successful performance of a skill is dependent on many variables, some of which the athlete controls, but many of which are beyond individual control. For example, the skill of returning a ball with a racquet is affected by the speed, direction, and spin of the oncoming ball, the playing surface and lighting, the receiver's eyesight, reaction speed, technique, and numerous other variables. Even if the receiver hits one successful return, the likelihood of the ball coming in exactly the same manner a second time is remote. Consequently, even with reinforcement for performing the skill correctly, unless the athlete has developed the skill to a high level of consistency, performance errors should be expected. With beginning athletes especially, coaches should be aware that positive reinforcement does not guarantee perfect performance.

Feedback as Negative Reinforcement

Feedback that serves as negative reinforcement possesses unpleasant properties that an athlete will avoid if at all possible. For feedback to serve as negative reinforcement, its removal or avoidance must strengthen the response you want your athlete to learn (see Figure 8.4).

An example of intrinsic feedback that may serve as negative reinforcement is the dissatisfaction of seeing the basketball you just shot miss the basket and of sensing kinesthetically that your body did not move as you intended it to move during the performance of the shot. Because intrinsic feedback can be very unpleasant, you will attempt to avoid it on future shots by changing your shooting technique. If the change results in intrinsic feedback that serves as positive reinforcement (the satisfaction of seeing the basketball go into the basket) and the removal of intrinsic feedback that acts as negative reinforcement (dissatisfaction of seeing the basketball miss the basket), the new technique is likely to become strengthened with practice and eventually learned.

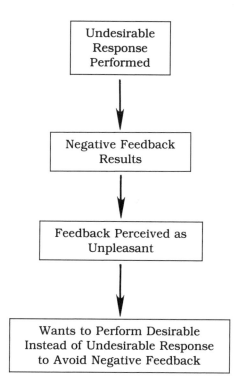

Figure 8.4 The desired response is strengthened when negative feedback is avoided or removed as a consequence of its performance.

Augmented feedback may also act as negative reinforcement. For instance, Mike, the coach of a youth league baseball team, was trying to improve Bob's batting. He had been trying to get Bob to be consistent in taking a shorter step with his leading leg as he swung at the pitch. Mike had talked to him about shortening the step, shown him films, and called out at him every time he made the mistake. Nothing seemed to work. Mike thought about the problem and decided he would try using negative reinforcement. He waited until the season had finished and then placed a wooden barrier on the ground about twelve inches in front of where Bob's left leg was striding. The wooden barrier, which was too high to step over when batting, was placed at the maximum distance that Bob should stride with his left leg when performing the skill correctly. At first Bob's left leg collided with the

barrier on each incorrect swing. Eventually Bob learned to cut down the length of his stride so that he did not hit the barrier. Avoiding the negative feedback of the barrier reinforced the shortened stride and increased the probability that he would keep it short when batting in the future.

Negative reinforcement should not be confused with punishment. Punishment involves causing an unpleasant situation for your athletes that occurs *after* the behavior in order to eliminate an undesirable behavior. For example, not allowing an athlete to play for the next two games because he or she missed a practice is a form of punishment. Because negative reinforcement involves removing an undesirable sensation that occurs as a consequence of your athlete's performance, the undesirable sensation requires a change in technique to remove it. Thus your athlete's skill is forced to improve in order to remove the negative reinforcer. Can you think of some ways negative reinforcement could be applied to your sport?

FEEDBACK AS PUNISHMENT TO ELIMINATE ERRORS

Like feedback used as negative reinforcement, feedback that functions as punishment also possesses unpleasant properties that an athlete will avoid if possible. In fact, the same unpleasant and aversive feedback can be used to produce either negative reinforcement or punishment, depending on whether it strengthens or weakens a response.

How Feedback Functions as Punishment

For feedback to act as punishment it must follow (preferably immediately) the response we want an athlete to eliminate or decrease the likelihood that the response will be repeated in the future under similar conditions. In other words, when feedback is presented to punish a response, it simply weakens it. Essentially, the punishing feedback is avoided by learning not to perform the response being punished, as shown in Figure 8.5.

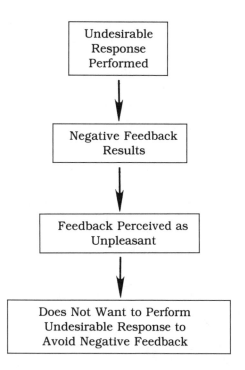

Figure 8.5   The undesirable response is weakened when negative feedback is given as a consequence of its performance.

An example of intrinsic feedback that may serve as punishment is the unpleasant experience of feeling a severe pain in your elbow each time you throw a certain pitch, such as the curve ball in baseball. This kind of intrinsic feedback is very offensive, so you will try to avoid it in the future by not throwing that particular pitch.

Of more importance in coaching is how augmented feedback may serve as punishment. As an example, suppose a basketball coach decides to use feedback as punishment to stop a player from repeatedly making the error of taking an unnecessary dribble (bounce) of the ball just prior to taking a shot. He could punish the error in a couple of ways. One way is to express (nonverbally and verbally) his or her disapproval of the unnecessary dribble immediately after the player performs it. Another way is for the coach to threaten to withdraw positive reinforcement immediately after the player makes the error. For instance, the coach could threaten (a) to take the player off the first team and put him or her on the second team or (b) to give him or her less playing time in games until he or she learns to eliminate the unnecessary dribble.

Regardless of which way feedback is used as punishment, however, it is important to note that the coach punished the undesirable action or error—the unnecessary dribble—and not the player. The problem with punishing the player is that it could cause him or her to feel rejected and, as a result, could produce emotions of resentment, aggression, hostility, or avoidance. On the other hand, if only the undesirable action is punished and effort is praised, the player can still feel liked and wanted and is likely to take the punishment in stride.

Unfortunately, some coaches use augmented feedback as punishment not for the good of the athlete or to eliminate performance errors but for the satisfaction they derive from punishing. They derive pleasure from dominating their athletes and using punishment to make them cringe. Some coaches become frustrated when their athletes fail to perform correctly and, in their frustration, use augmented feedback as punishment in an aggressive reaction to their athletes' errors. Other coaches thoughtlessly use physical activity, such as running laps or doing push-ups, as punishment. These practices can only increase the chance that the athlete will learn to resent the kinds of physical activity used as punishment rather than learning to enjoy them. These incorrect and ineffective uses of punishment should always be avoided; not only can they be very detrimental to the learning and performance of sport skills, but they can also take the fun out of participating for the athlete.

Guidelines for Using Augmented Feedback as Punishment

Augmented feedback as punishment to eliminate an unwanted action in the performance of a sport skill should be used sparingly and only when you think it is the only way to get the athlete to learn to perform the skill correctly. If using augmented feedback in other ways, such as knowledge, positive or negative reinforcement, or incentive, won't get rid of the undesirable action, then try it as punishment. Before you do, however, be certain that what you think of as punishment is not perceived by the athlete as positive reinforcement. What you think of as punishment may not be punishment for the athlete; it may be the attention that he or she desires. It is received when you punish the unwanted action and can be satisfying to the athlete and result in the unwanted action being strengthened by positive reinforcement instead of being weakened by the augmented feedback you intended as punishment. However, once you know that the athlete will perceive your augmented feedback as punishment, it is time to punish. There are four guidelines you should follow:

- Explain the situation to the athlete and warn him or her before you actually administer the punishment.
- Be serious and firm when you present the punishing augmented feedback but, most important, control your emotion. Refrain from punishing when you are upset and avoid giving punishment in a hostile manner. Don't criticize, shout, or sermonize; the consequences of this type of behavior can either reinforce (via attention) the very action you want to eliminate or cause the athlete to feel resentment, hostility, aggression, or the desire to escape from this unpleasant situation by quitting the team.
- Be consistent in your procedure of giving punishment and present it immediately after the action you want to eliminate.
- Use punishment only when necessary and always in conjunction with emphasizing the positive by complimenting, praising, and rewarding the athlete's effort to improve and correct his or her performance. Coaches frequently go wrong when trying to use punishment to eliminate an undesirable action because they forget to reinforce effort and correct performance or they show resentment or a grudge towards an athlete after he or she acts in the unwanted manner. Always accentuate the positive and make the athlete feel that he or she is a well-liked, valued member of the team.

FEEDBACK AS MOTIVATION FOR SKILL LEARNING

Feedback can have a strong influence on an athlete's motivation to learn new sports skills and refine or perform previously learned ones. By motivation we mean the internal mechanisms that arouse and direct our behavior. It involves both the availability of energy for use and the direction of the action or performance to some goal. Suppose an athlete's goal is to learn to perform a skill exactly as it was explained and demonstrated by the coach. Assume that the athlete, Jay, is motivated to achieve this goal because the coach convinced him that it is one prerequisite for fulfilling his need to feel competent, successful, worthy as a person, and to have fun. After each attempt to perform the skill, Jay receives intrinsic and augmented feedback that informs him about the distance of his present performance from the goal performance and how to correct the error. Knowing these factors enables him to modify his actions to reduce the difference between present performance and goal performance until eventually, through learning, they become identical. In this context feedback is providing knowledge that influences the directive function of the athlete's motivation.

Feedback can also have an effect on how much energy the athlete will expend on future attempts to perform a skill when trying to learn the goal performance. For example, if feedback (intrinsic or augmented) indicates that the difference between the athlete's present performance and the goal performance is less than it was on previous attempts to perform the skill, the athlete is likely to perceive that he or she is improving and that progress is being made. Feedback conveying this kind of information can be very satisfying to the athlete and act as an incentive to continue to use available energy to try to improve his or her present performance until the goal performance is finally learned. However, if the feedback reveals that the difference between present performance and the goal is unchanged or even more than it was on previous attempts to perform the skill, the athlete will probably think that little or no improvement or progress is taking place. Feedback carrying this message can be quite frustrating. It may serve as an incentive either to reduce the amount of energy used in future attempts to learn the goal performance or not to use any energy at all to learn it in the future. That is, the athlete may not try very hard to learn the skill or may completely give up trying.

USING AUGMENTED FEEDBACK AS POSITIVE REINFORCEMENT FOR SKILL SHAPING

You know how you would like your athlete to perform a skill. Unfortunately the athlete does not often perform it that way. How can you use augmented feedback to get the athlete to change the performance of the skill so that it conforms to your goal? One method for accomplishing this task is to utilize augmented feedback as positive reinforcement to shape the skill: You would positively reinforce closer and closer approximations of the correct skill performance. Beginners just learning a new skill and advanced athletes making a major change in technique are unlikely to perform the skill correctly at first, so any performance resembling the goal must be reinforced. After subsequent attempts, however, the requirements for giving augmented feedback as positive reinforcement become more exact and should only be given when the performance closely approximates correct skill performance. These are the steps of the shaping process:

1. *Define the correct skill performance.* For example, the handstand is held steady for at least 4 seconds and is performed unassisted with correct

form (head slightly tilted back, back slightly arched, legs together, knees straight, toes pointed, arms about shoulder-width apart, and palms of the hands flat on the mat with fingers spread).
2. *Identify an initial skill performance that is as close as possible to the correct skill performance.* The gymnast performed the handstand with the assistance of a spotter, but certain aspects of the form were not correct (legs were not together, knees were bent, and toes were not pointed).
3. *Develop steps of performance objectives that will take the athlete from the initial skill performance to the correct skill performance.*

   - Step 1: The gymnast, aided by a spotter, will be able to perform the handstand with legs together four times out of four attempts.
   - Step 2: The gymnast, aided by a spotter, will be able to perform the handstand with legs together and knees straight four times out of four attempts.
   - Step 3: The gymnast, aided by a spotter, will be able to perform the handstand with legs together, knees straight, and toes pointed four times out of four attempts.
   - Step 4: The gymnast will be able to hold the handstand steady at least four seconds and perform it unassisted with correct form four times out of four attempts.

4. *Identify the augmented feedback you think the athlete will perceive as positive reinforcement.* Verbal and nonverbal compliments, praise, and encouragement are identified. For example, you could use verbal feedback such as "That was super," "Well done," "That's it, now you've got it," or "That was perfect" and nonverbal feedback such as a smile, nod of approval, or pat on the back.
5. *Prepare the athlete for each step by giving him or her an idea of how to perform the skill at that step.* This is done

with an explanation and/or demonstration of what you want the gymnast to do at each step.

6. *Reinforce each step with augmented feedback until the skill performance specified by the performance objective for that step is reached.*
7. *Follow the series of steps until the correct skill performance is achieved.*

Shaping skill performance with augmented feedback is most effective when applied individually to athletes because the series of steps can be specifically designed according to the athlete's particular capabilities. However, a reasonable approximation of shaping can be achieved for many of the athletes on your team by establishing a sequence of performance objectives like the ones identified for the handstand or those discussed in chapter 1 to direct the group toward the correct skill performance. For example, the sacrifice bunt in baseball or a lay-up shot in basketball could be taught to beginners by designing a sequence of four to eight steps of performance objectives, each progressively more difficult and leading up to the correct performance.

One last point should be made about shaping. Although we have limited our discussion to shaping skill performance with augmented feedback, the same techniques can be used to develop other behaviors, such as good sportsmanship and knowledge of rules and strategies as well as positive personal qualities like self-discipline, cooperation, and emotional control. Furthermore, behavior shaping need not be used only with augmented feedback; it can also occur through intrinsic feedback that serves as a reinforcer.

USING AUGMENTED FEEDBACK FOR SKILL MODIFICATION

Whereas shaping attempts to develop skills an athlete did not previously learn, modification strives to change the rate of occurrence of skills already learned by an athlete. For example, suppose a player first learned the bad habit of bouncing a basketball once before each shot and then learned to correct it and

shoot without always bouncing the ball first. Both the bad habit and the correction have been learned. The problem is to make the correction more likely to occur than the bad habit. This can be accomplished by applying the basic principles of skill modification. Whether you want to increase the rate of occurrence of a correct performance or decrease the rate of occurrence of an incorrect performance, the basic principles involve the following:

1. Defining the skill performance you want to modify
2. Finding a form of augmented feedback that will be perceived by the athlete as a reinforcer or punisher
3. Determining the exact relationship between the skill performance and the consequence (establishing the contingency)
4. Applying the contingency
5. Observing the consequent change

Using Augmented Feedback to Increase a Desirable Performance

To increase the probability of a correct or desirable performance occurring, you can use augmented feedback. There are four strategies you can use to accomplish this goal:

- *Give augmented feedback that positively reinforces the correct skill performance.* Verbally praise your athletes when he or she perfoms the skill correctly.
- *Avoid all use of augmented feedback used previously to punish an incorrect performance.* No longer scold the player for performing the skill incorrectly.
- *Give augmented feedback that operates as negative reinforcement.* The player avoids being scolded for performing the skill incorrectly by performing it correctly.
- *Provide a model and give augmented feedback that reinforces the performance of the model.* Praise your athlete after he or she performs the skill in the desired way. Other athletes notice this praise and are thus encouraged to imitate the performance of the athlete who was praised.

Using Augmented Feedback to Decrease an Undesirable Performance

You can use augmented feedback to decrease the rate of occurrence of an incorrect or undesirable performance in the following manner:

- *Withdraw augmented feedback that acts as reinforcement.* A baseball team is told not to pay attention to or praise the undesirable show-off performance of one of the athletes on the team. The coach ignores it also.
- *Present augmented feedback that functions as punishment.* A baseball coach scolds a young pitcher who intentionally throws at a batter's head to back him or her away from home plate.
- *Give augmented feedback that positively reinforces an athlete for not making an error.* A coach compliments a player for not making a performance error that he or she almost always made before.

Final Remarks About Using Augmented Feedback to Modify Skill Performance

We have discussed the principal ways of using augmented feedback to increase or decrease the frequency of occurrence of a previously learned skill. However, you should take into account four additional factors as you attempt to modify an athlete's skill performance.

- The only way you can be certain that augmented feedback is operating the way you think it should is actually to try it—apply the contingency and observe the changes that take place.
- Always be aware that you are not the only one providing augmented feedback to an athlete after his or her performance. For example, suppose a baseball player is receiving augmented feedback from his or her two best friends on the team that positively reinforces flashy play at shortstop. At the same time the player is also receiving augmented feedback from the coach

that positively reinforces conservative, fundamental play at shortstop. Thus two sources of augmented feedback are operating as competing reinforcers. You must recognize that peer reinforcement may be stronger than the reinforcement from the coach.
- Modifying a skill performance in one situation is no guarantee that it will be modified in other situations. For instance, you may manage contingencies well enough that your athletes perform their skills very well in practices, but they perform them poorly in competition. One reason for this could be that the contingencies in practice are different from those in games. Your athletes thus develop different ways of playing in practices and in games. To resolve this problem utilize contingencies in practice as similar to those that operate in games as possible.
- Modifying a skill performance should follow a certain schedule of reinforcement. Early in the process of modifying a performance, reinforce correct performance with augmented feedback each time it occurs, just as you would in shaping a performance. However, after the athlete is performing the skill at the desired frequency, give the reinforcing augmented feedback less and less often.

SUMMARY AND RECOMMENDATIONS

Feedback is information your athletes receive as a consequence of their performance. Intrinsic feedback occurs as a natural consequence of performance; augmented feedback is added information that ordinarily is not available as a natural consequence of performance. If used effectively, feedback not only helps your athletes improve their skill performance but also helps them maintain it once a high level has been acquired. The secret to using feedback effectively is to understand how it functions as information-knowledge, reinforcement punishment, and motivation. The following list will help.

1. Feedback (intrinsic or augmented) that functions as information or knowledge mainly conveys a message about the overall effectiveness of a skill performance, the errors that were made, and how to correct them.
2. For feedback (intrinsic or augmented) to act as positive reinforcement, it must have pleasant properties and follow (preferably immediately) the response you want to strengthen.
3. For feedback (intrinsic or augmented) to serve as negative reinforcement it must have unpleasant and aversive properties that the athlete can avoid by making the response you want to strengthen.
4. For feedback (intrinsic or augmented) to function as punishment, it must have unpleasant and aversive properties and follow (preferably immediately) the response you want to suppress.
5. Feedback (intrinsic or augmented) can motivate athletes to learn skills if it provides information about their performance errors and how to correct them (directive function of motivation) and about their improvement in performance (arousal function of motivation).
6. Shaping that attempts to develop skills not previously learned by your athletes uses augmented feedback (verbal and nonverbal) as positive reinforcement of progressively closer approximations of the correct skill performance.
7. Modification attempts to change the rate of occurrence of previously learned skills. Increasing or decreasing the rate of occurrence of a performance involves (a) defining the performance you want to modify, (b) identifying the augmented feedback that will act as a reinforcer or punisher, (c) implementing the chosen contingency schedule, and (d) observing and evaluating effects.
8. Whether you use augmented feedback as knowledge about performance to correct errors, as positive reinforcement for skill shaping, or as reinforcement or punishment for skill modification, it should be given as often as possible early in learning and should gradually decrease in frequency as learning progresses.

Chapter 9
Analyzing Skills and Correcting Errors

The ability to analyze what an athlete is doing wrong and to know how to correct it is just as important as the ability to communicate this information to that athlete. Taken together, these are two of your most important teaching responsibilities as a coach. In this chapter you will learn how you can become effective at analyzing skills and providing feedback. We will discuss in detail the following topics:

- Analyzing skill technique
- Approaches to correcting errors
- Correcting skill errors in advanced athletes
- Developing an inner game approach

ANALYZING SKILL TECHNIQUE

Every athlete develops his or her own unique way of executing a skill. Even when all competitors perform the same skills, as, for example, in the compulsory routines in gymnastics and ice skating, athletes demonstrate their own subtle variations in technique. The uniqueness of an athlete's approach can complicate your analysis of technique. However, if you understand the basic principles of a particular skill, you should be able to help your athlete improve his or her own technique regardless of personal variations. When analyzing the technique of an athlete, try to (a) compare observed technique with correct technique, (b) select one error to correct at a time, and (c) determine the cause of the error and how to correct it.

Compare Observed Technique with Correct Technique

Novice coaches frequently make the mistake of watching a skill once and immediately offering corrections if the skill is not performed as described in the textbook. This approach runs the risk of failing to spot a fundamental error that is causing the mistake you observed and of focusing on a point that will have little impact on improving the athlete's performance. Before making suggestions to your athletes, take the time to observe and evaluate their technique. If you find an error, first decide if it needs correction. If the error is merely a reflection of the athlete's style, which is unusual but fundamentally sound, no useful purpose is served by correcting it. For example, what if one of your young wrestlers has adopted an unorthodox stance. Should you teach the correct technique or allow the wrestler to continue, without commenting on the stance? Similar situations occur regularly in all sports, often leaving the coach perplexed about how to respond. To resolve the situation ask yourself if the unorthodox technique is fundamentally sound. Numerous outstanding athletes have performed successfully using unusual, but fundamentally sound, personal styles. Baseball great Stan Musial had an unorthodox batting stance, but his baseball swing was fundamentally sound. Golfing greats Lee Trevino, Ray Floyd, and Miller Barber have somewhat unusual swings, but they consistently square-up the club at impact to produce successful performance results. Returning to our wrestling example, as long as the wrestler is able to move from the unorthodox stance to the positions necessary to take down opponents successfully and defend against being taken down, it may be better not to change the stance, even though you would not ordinarily recommend such a stance. You should correct the athlete only if sound offense and defense are precluded by this unusual stance.

Consider correcting technique if it is not fundamentally sound and if changing it will improve performance or increase safety. Football, for example, is a sport where safety is of primary concern, and the correct, head-up technique of teaching tackling is essential. The correct tackling technique will reduce the risk of injury and the successfulness of the athlete's personal tackling style is beside the point. In many outdoor sports safety concerns justify your insistence that individuals adhere strictly to the correct technique. Examine your sport to determine if individual variation is acceptable or if strict adherence to textbook technique is essential.

Select One Error to Correct at a Time

How should you respond when you notice several errors in technique after watching one of your athletes perform a skill? Should you correct each error? Should you correct just one error? Should you correct only the most critical errors? If you've played golf, you'll know that a faulty swing can be due to an incorrect stance, incorrect leg and body movement, faulty alignment, an incorrect grip, and several other possible technique-related problems. Where do you begin?

Like a detective sifting through a mass of clues to solve the crime, the coach has to identify the crux of the performance problem. One error is often the cause of others so you can correct the situation by identifying and eliminating the critical error. In our golf example, the stance is faulty, the leg and body movements will probably be incorrect as a result, and adjusting the stance may eliminate the incorrect leg and body movements. Remember, therefore, to look first for the critical error, the correction of which may eliminate the other errors.

When the errors seem unrelated, correct the one that is easiest to learn and will result in the greatest improvement. Even very small improvements will enhance your athletes' motivation to continue striving to upgrade their skills. For example, you may notice that one of your right-handed softball players is consistently making two batting errors and consequently missing the ball. The first error is turning the head on the swing and not watching the ball; the correction is to keep the head still and to watch the ball until contact is made. The second error, often called a hitch, occurs just before the forward stride of the front leg and the onset of the forward swing of the bat: The batter shifts the hands downward then upward. Which error should the coach correct first?

Most coaches would agree that the movement of the head should be corrected first because (a) it is the easiest to correct and (b) being a successful hitter is almost impossible if the head is not kept reasonably still with the player's eyes focused on the ball. As the coaching maxim says, "You can't hit what you can't see." Although the hitch in the swing is a batting error, players who keep the head still and watch the ball closely can be successful despite this flaw.

The time factor may help you focus your skills analysis. Some skills, like the javelin throw, take several seconds to perform; others take split seconds, such as swerving or sidestepping by a running back in football. For skills that last several seconds, you should identify the important error that occurs earliest in the sequence. For example, in the javelin throw and long jump, if the run-up is technically incorrect, the rest of the skill is likely to be incorrectly performed. Another error-correcting principle is to work from the base of support upwards, which is useful in a sport like gymnastics that requires good balance. If your athletes have not positioned their limbs correctly to provide a sound base, their movements will be off balance.

In some situations the errors will seem unrelated to each other, and none will appear to take precedence in time or importance. When this occurs, consider letting your athletes choose the error they would like to correct first. Involving your athletes in the error-correction process can make the suggested changes more meaningful to them and may motivate them to try harder than they would simply following your instructions. You may be surprised to discover that sometimes the athlete knows better than you where to begin.

Determine the Cause of the Error and How to Correct It

After selecting the error needing correction, determine its cause and the appropriate remedy. This process can be relatively easy, as when an athlete's technique is incorrect because he or she forgot to concentrate on a particular part of the skill. For instance, if a coach determines that a young gymnast is forgetting to point his or her toes during the handstand, the correction is simple—remind the gymnast to concentrate on pointing the toes and ask that the skill be repeated correctly. In this instance

- forgetting is the *cause* of the error,
- failing to point the toes is the *error*, and
- reminding the gymnast to point the toes is the *correction*.

When forgetting causes an error, a reminder of the desired technique is sufficient in most situations to produce the necessary correction. If an athlete consistently forgets a key point despite your reminders, however, you should suspect that another factor is causing the problem. Has the athlete not fully understood your instructions? Does he or she possess the prerequisite skill level? You must examine all possible performance clues to ascertain the answers.

Determining the cause and the correction can be very difficult indeed. Consider, for example, a coach who saw his right-handed pitcher consistently throwing the baseball too high to the batter. The coach correctly identified a pitching problem and sought the remedy. He decided that the pitcher was releasing the ball too soon and told the pitcher to hold onto it longer before the release. The pitcher tried the correction again and again but without success. Why didn't it work? The coach had made a common error: treating the symptom instead of the cause. Further analysis of the pitcher's technique during the practice revealed the actual cause of the error; the pitcher was overstriding with the left foot when stepping toward home plate to deliver the pitch. To correct this error, the pitcher had to learn to shorten the length of stride of the left leg.

When you are uncertain about the cause of an error or how to correct it, think through the situation very carefully before making any suggestions. Watch the performance several times before deciding what to say. If you experiment with suggestions that do not lead to improved technique and performance, you may damage your credibility and frustrate your athletes.

Gary Wiren (1968) illustrates the value of waiting until you determine the cause of an error before making a correction. He relates a story concerning the great golfer Bobby Jones and his Scottish coach, Stewart Maiden. Jones was practicing for the U. S. Open Golf Tournament several days before the event but was not hitting the ball very accurately and was unable to diagnose and correct the error. He quickly telephoned Maiden and asked him to come and help. When Maiden arrived they went straight to the practice area, and Maiden without saying a word, watched Jones hit ball after ball without very much success. After two buckets of balls had been errantly stroked, Maiden said in his abrupt and rough Scottish manner, "Why dintya tri itting it an yer backswing?" (p. 53). At first Jones was puzzled by Maiden's question but after thinking about it for a few moments, he got the message. Jones slowed his backswing and immediately began to hit accurate shots once again.

What had Maiden done? He observed, evaluated, and thoroughly analyzed Jones' technique and performance before giving him any feedback. Maiden could have been less curt, more pleasant, and direct by politely and simply telling Jones to slow his backswing. However, Bobby Jones understood Maiden's style and accepted his advice. He also went on to finish tied for first in the U. S. Open.

Maiden did not confuse Jones with a detailed explanation of how to correct his error. Neither did he search about blindly for the proper correction by having Jones try a number of different corrections in his swing. Through rigorous, analytic thinking he isolated the proper correction and delivered the message to Jones in a way Jones could understand. This last point should be stressed—most athletes will be less experienced than Jones and need information feedback that is unambiguous and simple to understand. This is especially true for young athletes. Short, simple sentences containing a message that is easy to understand and without sarcasm provide the most useful feedback.

APPROACHES TO CORRECTING ERRORS

Some coaches have never been heard to utter one encouraging remark throughout their careers; other coaches seem to be full of encouragement regardless of the situation. The first type of coach illustrates the negative approach to correcting errors, whereas the second has developed a positive approach. Before reading the next section ask yourself: "Do I correct errors with a negative or positive approach?"

We recently observed a volunteer Little League coach trying to help a boy with his hitting. The youngster made a reasonably good swing on his first attempt but missed the ball. The coach had a look of displeasure on his face as he yelled, "Don't take your eyes off the ball when you swing!" On the next pitch the boy tried hard to keep his eyes on the ball; he kept his head very still and fouled the ball off. "Don't take such a big stride when you swing!" shouted the coach. On the next pitch, which was too high to hit, the boy made a sincere effort to follow both instructions but missed the ball again. The coach shook his head from side to side to indicate a *no* and then stated, "You're making one mistake after another. What's wrong with you? Don't you

know the strike zone? Don't swing at bad pitches!"

On the next pitch the boy concentrated on all three instructions but popped the ball up in the infield. The coach was really frustrated now. He not only shook his head but looked down and away from the boy. After a moment of silence, the coach yelled: "You're getting worse instead of better. I don't think you're ever going to learn to hit the ball. Now you're swinging up it."

The boy's reactions showed that he was not having fun. The look on his face said that he was disappointed and frustrated, and his baseball enthusiasm was quickly fading. He wanted to please his coach and was trying to think of all the things the coach had told him, but all this thinking now seemed to make him less confident and more hesitant about swinging at any pitch. He was becoming mechanical, slower, and the coordination he had displayed on the first swing was beginning to disappear.

Have you ever used this kind of approach? What can we learn from this story? Did the coach not know what he was talking about? In fact, he did not. Although the coach correctly identified the youngster's errors, he failed in the manner he used to correct the errors. He exemplified a negative approach.

Negative Approach to Correcting Errors

We discussed earlier the tendency to react to the symptoms instead of the causes of errors in your athletes' techniques. The coach in the Little League example pointed out every fault in technique but never gave the athlete the information needed to perform the skill successfully. The coach's inability to identify the actual cause of the problem is one possible reason for the athlete's failure. But the coach had an additional failing: His entire approach to the athlete was negative and was based on the assumption that performance errors were occurring because the athlete was not concentrating or trying hard enough. This approach further assumes that errors are without value and, perhaps most important when young athletes are concerned, fails to acknowledge the sincere efforts made in trying to correct performance. Finally, it focuses more on what not to do than on what to do and reacts to errors using ridicule, sarcasm, excessive criticism, and punishment. This approach creates fear of failure and promotes self-doubt in athletes.

The undesirable consequences of the negative approach cannot be overemphasized. You may not be such a coach, but too many individuals in coaching are. Whenever you see coaches using the negative approach, if you think they might be receptive to your observations, don't hesitate to say that this approach does *not* help athletes improve their skills. Suggest taking a positive approach.

Positive Approach to Correcting Errors

The baseball coach would have had more success if—instead of pointing out one error after another in a hostile manner—he had smiled at his athlete and in a friendly and reassuring voice said, "Nice try, that was a good swing, but you could do better if you watch the ball closely when you swing." This is a positive approach. It assumes that errors are inevitable and will occur as a natural part of the skill-learning process. Errors are viewed as important because they indicate the level of athlete performance in comparison with where it should be, and this information is necessary for corrective action. Errors are valuable because they are part of the learning process.

The positive approach emphasizes what to do instead of what not to do and uses compliments, praise, rewards, corrective information, and encouragement more than punishment. Correct performance and improvement are acknowledged, and efforts made in striving to improve are complimented. If used wisely, the positive approach can help your athletes feel good about themselves and promote a strong desire to achieve.

When you are working with one athlete at a time, the positive approach to correcting errors consists of the following instructional steps:

1. Praise effort and correct performance.
2. Give simple and precise corrective feedback.
3. Verify that the corrective feedback is understood.
4. Motivate the athlete to use the corrective feedback.

These steps utilize the material discussed in chapter 8. In Step 1 you are using augmented feedback to positively reinforce the effort and performance you want from the athlete. In Step 2 you are using augmented feedback to provide knowledge about the parts of the skill that were performed correctly as well as incorrectly and how to correct the errors. In Step 3 you are making certain that the message you sent in Step 2 was received and understood by the athlete so that he or she can apply it when resuming practice of the skill. In Step 4 you are encouraging the athlete to use the corrective feedback with the intent to improve.

You should incorporate the positive approach to correcting errors, but be certain to use these four steps only as a sequence of guidelines to help you communicate in a positive and constructive way with each of your athletes. Be yourself and use your own special personal style and communication skills to carry out each of the four steps. Moreover, be sure to consider the unique personality and needs of the athlete with whom you are working. For example, if you tend to be a stern coach, displaying little emotion, communicating best verbally and concisely, then carry out the four steps in that manner. However, don't overlook the needs of your athletes. For example, one athlete might need to be praised (positively reinforced) for effort each time he or she attempts to perform a skill, whereas another may respond better if praised for effort only once in awhile (Step 1). Similarly, you may have to emphasize Step 4 when working with an athlete who needs to be motivated but practically ignore it with someone highly self-motivated to achieve. In some situations you may not need to repeat all four steps each time the athlete performs the skill. Let's look more closely at each of these very important steps.

Step 1: Praise Effort and Correct Performance.

Praise your athlete for trying to perform the skill correctly and for performing any parts of the skill properly. As a general rule, give your praise as soon as possible after the athlete performs the skill. Keep it simple rather than elaborate. Examples of simple verbal praise for effort are ''Good try,'' ''Nice hustle,'' ''You couldn't have tried any harder,'' or ''You gave it your best shot, and that's all anyone can ask.'' Examples of simple verbal praise for correct performance are ''Your form was super,'' ''You sure did a lot of things right,'' ''You really kept your head still on the swing, and that's what I want,'' or ''Now you've got it; your weight is over the balls of your feet where it should be.'' In addition to verbal feedback, don't forget to use positive nonverbal feedback, such as clapping your hands, smiling, or any facial or bodily expressions showing that you approve of the effort and correct performance.

Be sincere and honest with your praise. Do not indicate that an athlete's effort was good when it was not. In most instances an athlete knows when he or she has made a sincere effort to perform the skill correctly and perceives undeserved praise for what it is—untruthful feedback to make him or her feel good. Likewise, do not indicate that an athlete's performance was correct when it was not. If the athlete is near the end of the intermediate stage of learning or in the advanced stage, he or she will know when the skill or parts of it were performed incorrectly and perceive the praise as being undeserved. If the athlete is in the beginning stage of learning or the early part of the intermediate stage, he or she will not yet be able to distinguish between correct and incorrect performance, and praising an incorrect performance at this stage to avoid hurting the youngster's feelings could lead to learning incorrect movements.

Although the positive approach places emphasis on using praise more than criticism, this does not mean that you should avoid giving an athlete augmented feedback that provides knowledge about how the performance was incorrect or that expresses your displeasure with his or her effort to learn or perform a skill. Augmented feedback including these kinds of criticisms are important to communicate to your athletes. However, when you deliver critical augmented feedback, you should be in control and do so in a firm but moderate way. Like elaborate praise, strong or severe criticism is unlikely to promote achievement in your athletes; criticism delivered in a moderate way is much more effective.

Step 2: Give Simple and Precise Corrective Feedback.

In this step augmented feedback is being used mainly to provide knowledge about performance errors and how to correct them. Before providing this kind of feedback, find out when your athletes are likely to be most receptive to receiving it. Some of your athletes will readily accept it immediately after a performance, and others will not. Some athletes respond best to immediate correction, and feedback is particularly meaningful to them at that time. However, other athletes respond much better to corrective feedback if it is slightly delayed, which allows them to calm down, think things over for themselves, and respond to the corrective feedback less emotionally and more objectively.

Major performance errors that are complicated to explain and understand and difficult to correct can be addressed in the following manner:

1. Explain and demonstrate what the athlete has done (error) in comparison with what should have been done (correction).
2. Explain the cause or causes of the error (if not obvious).
3. Explain why you are recommending the correction you have selected (if not obvious).

Knowing the causes of an error and your reasons for recommending one correction rather than another will help your athletes more thoroughly understand their error and what has to be done to correct it. Explicitly understanding these factors can increase the rate of learning for beginners and can be used by advanced performers subsequently to correct related errors without the assistance of their coach. In addition, it can motivate your athletes to try the correction you recommended because they are allowed to know the rationale underlying your feedback. Some of these procedures will not be needed to correct simple errors. For instance, the failure of a gymnast to point his or her toes when doing a handstand requires you only to inform the athlete about the correction to be made. You will, of course, have to use judgment in these situations, but the material in this chapter should prove a useful guide.

Regardless of the level of complexity of the error and correction, be careful not to burden your athlete with excessively long or detailed information. Give just enough feedback so he or she can concentrate on correcting one error at a time. Furthermore, present the information at a speed that will enable the athlete to understand it and to translate it into the movement that will result in making the correction. There are many other details to consider when performing this step, but they have been discussed previously (see chapters 3, 4, 5, and 8) and will not be included here. However, a brief review of the content of these chapters should convince you that completing this second step is relatively effortless.

Step 3: Verify the Athlete's Understanding of the Corrective Feedback.

Now that you have presented corrective feedback to your athlete, you need to find out if he or she has understood it. Remember, communication consists of not only sending messages but also receiving and understanding them. If the athlete doesn't understand the corrective feedback you presented in Step 2, he or she will continue to perform the skill incorrectly. One means of verifying the athlete's understanding is to ask him or her to repeat the corrective feedback just presented and to explain and demonstrate how it will be used when practice resumes. If the athlete is unable to do so, be patient and understanding. Present the corrective feedback again and have the athlete repeat it. If it is understood at this point, answer any final questions the athlete may have.

Step 4: Motivate the Athlete to Strive to Improve.

Before the athlete returns to practice encourage him or her to strive to improve his or her skill performance by learning the correction you recommended. Use words and actions that are designed to persuade the athlete to ''hang tough'' or persevere when corrections are difficult to learn and he or she is likely to become discouraged. In situations where improvement is not likely to occur quickly, assure the athlete that it will come about in time by practicing the corrections you recommended. But remind the athlete that it will come about only if he or she practices with the intent to improve. In addition, provide extra encouragement to athletes who lack self-confidence. You might say, ''You've made a great improvement in keeping your eyes on the ball today. With more practice, you will be hitting the ball much more consistently.'' The purpose of this step is to motivate the athlete to continue to learn and refine his or her skill.

CORRECTING ERRORS IN ADVANCED ATHLETES

Why is it difficult for athletes in the advanced stage of learning to make certain skill corrections? That is, why are some corrections easy but others much harder to make? Let's examine this problem in more detail.

Making skill corrections requiring little or no learning and replacing old skill components with new ones takes place quite easily, quickly, and with little or no adverse effect on performance. For example, having a softball player spread his or her feet apart more to correct a narrow batting stance can be accomplished quickly, without having to practice and learn anything; effects on batting performance tend to be almost completely positive. Furthermore, corrections requiring a minimum amount of learning are somewhat harder to make but can be accomplished without undue difficulty or negative performance effect. For instance, if a softball player repeatedly makes the mistake of taking his or her eyes off the ball during the swing because the head is turning with the swing, the error can be corrected during batting practice by having the player concentrate on keeping the head still during the swing. The coach need only emphasize watching the ball all the way to the plate and seeing the bat make contact. This correction will be somewhat more difficult to make than simply widening a batting stance—learning to concentrate on watching the ball is slightly more involved than replacing a narrow stance with a wider stance. Nevertheless, it can be made in a reasonable amount of time without adversely affecting batting.

On the other hand, making corrections that require a substantial amount of learning can be difficult; they should be approached carefully because unanticipated consequences can be devastating. Consider the case of Marty Fleckman. Some years ago he nearly won the U. S. Open golf championship as an amateur, and the following year he won the first professional tournament he entered. Marty subsequently began making corrections to perfect his golf swing that required a substantial amount of learning. As a result, his performance went into a permanent decline. He was never again a threat to win on the professional tour.

Although some golfers have succeeded at making this type of major correction in their swings, none have done so without paying a price. One famous example is Ben Hogan. He practiced for many years to correct his swing in an effort to perfect it and thus get it to hold up under the pressure of competition. A more recent example is Hubert Green, who in 1979 tried to make a correction in his swing to hit the ball higher and longer. The correction not only failed but prevented him from returning to his old, quite effective swing—or any other that worked—for several years. By 1983 he was finally able to learn a swing that worked and consequently won the prestigious Professional Golfers Association Tournament that year.

When you ask athletes to make a correction in a skill that requires a substantial amount of learning, you are essentially asking them to change their motor program for the skill. They will have to renegotiate the three stages of learning, discussed in chapter 2. They will return to the beginning stage of learning and then once again progress through the intermediate and advanced stages by practicing the skill until it is highly developed. How long this takes and how much performance is affected depends on

- the amount of practice needed to learn the correction by itself;
- the amount and type of transfer of learning that occurs between the previously learned incorrect part and the correction that will replace it (transfer of learning was discussed in chapter 7); and
- the amount of practice needed to learn to integrate the correction with the previously learned correct parts that will be retained so that the whole skill is performed in an automatic way.

As the amount of negative transfer of learning (interference) and the amount of practice needed to learn the correction and integrate it increases, the more time it takes to master the corrected skill, and the more performance is adversely affected. On the other hand, as the amount of positive transfer of learning (facilitation) increases and the amount of practice needed to learn the correction and integrate it decreases, the less time it takes to master the corrected skill, and the less performance is adversely affected.

Before attempting to suggest major skill corrections for an athlete, you ought to be able to respond positively to the following three questions:

- Is the athlete capable of making the correction?
- Is there enough time to make the correction?
- Is the athlete motivated to make the correction?

Is the Athlete Capable of Making the Correction?

In your judgment, does the athlete have the physical, intellectual, and emotional abilities necessary to make the correction successfully? Is the athlete physically capable? For example, his or her body build or flexibility may not be suitable for the changes in technique you are recommending. Is the athlete receptive and a fast learner? Some athletes are more receptive than others to trying a coach's suggestions for changing technique. Similarly, some athletes learn at faster rates than others.

No magic formula exists to help you find the answers to these and other questions that could be asked about the athlete's abilities. The answers will be based mainly on your judgment, but don't hesitate to seek the advice of more experienced coaches who may have faced a similar challenge. Regardless of which questions you ask and how they are answered, your final decision about whether or not an athlete is capable of making major corrections in his or her technique should be thoroughly thought through before you discuss it with the athlete.

Is There Enough Time to Make the Correction?

How long will it take the athlete to correct his or her technique? Can the correction be made before the first competition, or isn't that a concern? Is this the type of correction that could take a year or longer to perfect? If the answer to the latter question is yes, will the athlete be on the team or competing long enough after the correction is perfected to reap the benefits from it? Or will the athlete be near the end of his or her athletic career once the new technique is perfected? Once again, we advise you to seek the advice of more experienced coaches and use your judgment in answering these questions. Whatever decision you reach, however, consider it in detail before discussing the correction with the athlete.

Is the Athlete Motivated to Make the Correction?

Assuming the athlete is capable and time is sufficient, it is time to discuss your recommendations with the athlete and to motivate him or her to follow your advice. Once the corrections are understood, explain why you think they are necessary and, moreover, how performance will be improved. In addition, tell the athlete what is likely to happen when he or she attempts to relearn the technique. Make clear the fact that the athlete will have to return to the beginning stage of learning and develop a new motor program, which will take a considerable amount of time and practice. Indicate how much time and practice you think will be needed to perfect the corrections. Finally, explain the performance consequences that are likely to occur during relearning; that

is, performance will get worse before it gets better, and it will not be as proficient as it was when the old technique was being employed. However, when relearning is accomplished and the new motor program is developed, performance should be better than it was with the old technique.

If the athlete understands your recommendation and is motivated to make a major correction in technique, you should be aware of the possibility that he or she may hold you responsible for poor performance while relearning is taking place. If this occurs, you should be prepared to accept the blame where appropriate and take the pressure off the athlete because a relearning phase can be very discouraging and frustrating. Thus, be prepared to give the athlete your complete support and plenty of encouragement while he or she is learning to make a major correction in technique.

DEVELOPING AN INNER GAME APPROACH

The old adage, analysis leads to paralysis, seems particularly apt to describe the behavior of athletes learning sport skills. Why does performance suffer when athletes try too hard or think too much? According to Gallwey (1974), who popularized the inner-game concept, the cause is the fact that your athletes have two selves: Self 1 and Self 2. Self 1 is the conscious mind; it provides the instructional voice that attempts to direct, criticize, and question the actions of the body. For example, it might say to a 200-meter sprinter, "Relax your left arm as you run around the turn." Self 2, on the other hand, resembles a computer that monitors the body's natural feedback and carries out movements specified by the motor program, without the athlete's conscious participation.

Gallwey suggests that the more Self 2 can operate without the influence of Self 1, the better performance will be. How can you teach athletes to perform without paying conscious attention to what they are doing? The answer is to change the type of feedback to which they are attending. For example, tennis players evaluate their shots as good or bad and then concentrate on improving various aspects of technique. They might consider whether the wrist is too loose, the elbow correctly angled, the feet properly positioned and so on. This process involves Self 1. The alternative approach is to concentrate more on the outcome of the skill. Tennis coaches might tell their players to report how many feet a ball was from the baseline and not to use conscious error correction to perform the skill again. The idea is that the body will detect the differences between one swing and another and adjust the swing so that the ball lands in play. This approach utilizes Self 2.

A very important feature of stressing Self 2 is that the emphasis is on knowing what is actually happening, not on what should be happening. Gallwey has instructed players to verbalize the bounce-hit-bounce-hit sequence of the ball. By concentrating on this sequence, players in turn concentrate on the outcome of the stroke rather than executing it. This alteration of focus helps the athletes become much more aware of how accurate the performance is so that the next stroke is closer to the ideal performance.

Your athletes may also benefit from this approach in actual contest situations. In high jumping, for example, it is much better to concentrate on going over the bar than on what your legs and arms are doing. Similarly, when your players are batting, have them concentrate intently on the ball and let the swing take care of itself. Take care when teaching your athletes not to overemphasize the techniques involved in performing skills. Sometimes a more simple approach that encourages the body to adapt naturally to the environment will lead to more impressive results.

SUMMARY AND RECOMMENDATIONS

In this chapter you learned how to analyze your athletes' skills and how to use the positive approach when providing feedback to correct errors. You also learned how to approach making skill corrections in athletes who are in the advanced stage of learning. Finally, you learned about getting your athletes to develop an inner-game approach. The following ideas may be helpful in your coaching efforts:

1. To analyze a skill you must

   • compare the athlete's technique with the correct technique,
   • select one error to correct at a time,
   • determine the cause of the error, and
   • determine the correction of the error.

2. Consider changing technique only if the current technique is not fundamentally sound and a change will improve performance or increase safety.

3. The negative approach to correcting errors, which is not recommended, operates on the assumption that errors are bad and without value. It also fails to acknowledge a sincere effort and places more emphasis on what not to do than on what to do. This approach relies heavily on ridicule, sarcasm, excessive criticism, and punishment in response to an athlete's errors.

4. The positive approach to correcting errors, which we recommend, operates on the assumption that errors are a natural part of the skill-learning process and coaches and athletes alike can learn from them. It acknowledges a sincere effort and places more emphasis on what to do than on what not to do. This approach relies heavily on compliments, praise, rewards, corrective information, and encouragement in response to an athlete's errors.

5. The positive approach to correcting an athlete's error consists of the following instructional steps:

   • Praise effort and correct performance.
   • Give simple and precise corrective feedback.
   • Verify that the corrective feedback is understood.
   • Motivate the athlete to use the corrective feedback.

6. When employing the positive approach, use your own personal style and communication skills to carry out each of the four instructional steps, but do so in relation to the unique personality and needs of the athlete with whom you are working at the moment.

7. Making corrections in a well-learned technique that requires a substantial amount of learning is difficult to accomplish and should be approached carefully and systematically because the result can be a deterioration in performance.

8. For athletes to make a correction that requires a substantial amount of learning, they must change their motor program for the skill. To do this they must return to the beginning stage of learning and once again progress through the intermediate and advanced stages.

9. An increase in (a) the amount of negative transfer of learning (interference) and (b) the amount of practice needed to learn the correction and integrate it with previously learned parts causes a corresponding increase in the time it takes to acquire the corrected skill and decrease in performance.

10. Before attempting to make major skill corrections in one of your athletes you should be able to respond positively to the following three questions:

   • Is the athlete capable of making the correction?
   • Is there enough time to make the correction?
   • Is the athlete motivated to make the correction?

11. Some of your athletes may find it helpful to develop an inner-game approach in which they concentrate on what is to be done instead of how it is to be done.

PART IV
Cognitive Processes Involved in Skills

The last part of this book will deal with four of the cognitive processes that can affect your athletes' skill performance regardless of whether they are in the beginning, intermediate, or advanced stage of learning. These processes are imagery, memory, attention, and anticipation, which are covered in chapters 10, 11, 12, and 13, respectively. In these four chapters we will discuss how each cognitive process can function to affect your ath-letes' skill performance. This will help you understand and explain why your athletes are performing a certain way and will put you in a better position to teach your athletes how to improve. We also will suggest things you can do in your teaching and coaching to help your athletes use their cognitive processes effectively so that they can perform as proficiently as possible.

Chapter 10
Using Imagery to Improve Performance

Think of a sport that you have never participated in, close your eyes, and try to visualize yourself executing one of its skills. Then think of the sport that you perform best and visualize yourself performing one of its skills. Which did you find easier? Was it the image of the skill in which you are proficient? Do you think that if you mentally practiced visualizing performance and feeling the movements, your performance of the skill would improve?

Many coaches and athletes believe that practicing sport skills by using imagery can improve learning and performance. Although they are correct, it is important to realize that skills are not learned through imagery alone. Imagery can be very helpful if used properly, but it will not take the place of physically practicing the skill.

Imagery is sometimes described as *mental practice*, and the terms are frequently used interchangeably. We will use the term *imagery* in this chapter, however, because we think it more accurately represents the total involvement of the senses.

In this chapter we will focus on how imagery influences the learning and performance of motor skills. A comprehensive explanation of how imagery works, how you can improve your imagery skills, and how imagery affects behaviors other than motor skills is presented in the *Coaches Guide to Sport Psychology* (Martens, 1987). This chapter includes discussion of

- imagery and its use at different stages of learning,
- different ways to use imagery,
- principles for the successful use of imagery,

- when to use imagery, and
- where to use imagery.

IMAGERY AND ITS USE AT DIFFERENT STAGES OF LEARNING

When you imagined yourself performing the sport skills at the start of this chapter, you were using a form of visual imagery. The experience of using imagery is similar to sensory experiences like seeing, feeling, and hearing but is unique because it can occur without any external stimuli. When imaging batting technique, for example, there is no real baseball bat or pitcher, and you cannot actually see or hear the pitch as it comes toward you. The feel of the bat as you swing and your sense of movement as you round the bases after lining the ball are not really taking place. However, you can create the mental components, the images, of these sensory experiences in the absence of the actual events.

Imagery usually involves more than just the visual sense. Although the visual sense may be most acute, imagery can include auditory and tactile senses. With practice, athletes can develop the ability not only to see the imagined skill but also to hear and feel it. Feeling may include sensation of touch, muscular tensions and forces, and the body's orientation in space.

In chapter 2 we discussed how athletes pass through three stages of learning: beginning, intermediate, and advanced. The technique of using imagery is likely to be most effective in the intermediate and advanced stages of learning. However, let's examine its role in each of the three stages.

Beginning Stage

Unquestionably, observing skilled performers or listening to instructions can give athletes in the beginning stage of learning enough of an idea of how to perform the skill that they can image it. However, research evidence indicates that imagery is most helpful when your athletes have a reasonable idea of what the skill looks and feels like and the motor program is established. Although imagery can help beginners learn how the skill should look, it is of limited assistance in helping them develop the vital kinesthetic (movement) sense for the skill. This sense is most effectively developed through the actual performance of the skill. Until athletes have performed a skill a number of times, they will have no feeling for a correct performance and will not be able to image it effectively. They will also have difficulty using imagery because they will not know which parts of the skill to image. Practice through imagery should not be encouraged until the athletes have a reasonable idea of what the skill looks and feels like.

One situation in which imagery may be helpful when initially learning skills is combining a series of known skills into a new, more complex movement. For example, imagine you are trying to teach a young athlete the sequence of steps in a floor exercise routine in gymnastics. One way to use imagery would be to say something like, "Remember how you perform each step? You take a European hurdle, round off, and do a back handspring. See Sally [a respected model] perform those skills. Did you notice her form? Try to copy that form when you are performing your routine." To reinforce this advice you might have your athletes close their eyes for a moment and visualize the perfect performance before trying it themselves. Perhaps you can think of similar ways to use imagery in your sport with a beginning group of athletes.

Intermediate Stage

As you become more experienced in teaching your athletes to use imagery to learn and perform skills, you should strive to find the correct balance between the use of imagery and physical practice. You may find that learning skills is more effective if you use a combination of these two forms of practice than it would be using physical practice alone. Because there are many occasions on which physical practice is either impossible or undesirable (injury, inclement weather conditions, etc.), imagery can be a valuable supplement to an athlete's training program.

Teach athletes in the intermediate learning stage to use their imagery skills to keep the correct way to perform the skill vividly implanted in mind. Because many of you will have never used imagery before, either during your own athletic participation or in your coaching, you should try the following exercise. Select a specific skill from the sport you coach, such as the jump shot in basketball, a penalty kick in soccer, or a backhand slap shot in ice hockey. Imagine yourself performing the activity at the place where your athletes normally practice (gymnasium, playing field, ice rink, etc.). Close your eyes for about one minute and try to see yourself at this facility. Hear the sounds. Feel your body perform the skill. Concentrate on the experience.

You may have found this exercise easy, difficult, or even impossible. Your athletes will experience the same feelings. If they have difficulty imaging, you will have to spend some time teaching them how to image successfully. A variety of methods for teaching your athletes how to develop imagery skills are presented in detail in the *Coaches Guide to Sport Psychology* (Martens, 1987) and its accompanying *Study Guide*. It is important, however, to realize that imagery practice becomes much easier after it is practiced for a time on a systematic basis.

Advanced Stage

Imagery can be very effective once a skill has been well learned. The time of the season and type of skill should influence the way in which you combine the use of imagery and physical practice. Let us consider how long-distance running coach JoAnne, sprint coach Dennis, and baseball pitching coach Fred might use imagery with their athletes at various times of the season in their different sports.

Although all three coaches emphasize physical practice in the off season, they also advise their athletes to reserve some time for practicing imagery skills. Remember that imagery itself is a skill. If your athletes stop imaging for a period of time, they will lose some of their capacity to generate vivid and controlled images.

During the competitive season, JoAnne continues to place major emphasis on physical practice because long-distance runners need to spend a great deal of their time running to achieve high levels of conditioning. However, she also teaches them how to use imagery strategies during their running sessions to help stay relaxed.

The training for sprinters is quite different. Because the start is so important for successful racing and is always carried out when the athlete is not fatigued, Dennis does not want his sprinters performing starts while either mentally or physically tired. He therefore waits 5 minutes between each practice of the start. Because the actual sprint takes about 10 seconds, plenty of time is available between starts for his athletes to image all the key points of the start and to focus on specific aspects of the skill that need improvement. In addition imagery for sprinters might include concentrating on relaxing. Many runners have found that relaxation, rather than conscious effort, is the key to successful running. This principle applies to all sports in which running is a significant component.

Fred has a different problem, however. His pitchers always need several days to recover after pitching. He has learned that this recovery period is an excellent time in which to use imagery. For example, Fred often sits down with one of his pitchers and tells him to image pitching to a specific player in a specific situation in the game; he then tells his pitcher to image pitching to the next batter on the opponent's roster. Fred believes that if his pitcher has mentally practiced three successful pitches in the bottom of the ninth, bases loaded, one out, and his team leading by only one run, it will help his pitcher stay calm when this situation arises in a real game. In general, imagery should help pitchers concentrate well with runners on base and the opposition trying to intimidate the pitcher.

Imagery to control anxiety can be used in numerous sports. Those of you who teach tennis, for example, know that different stages of a match are accompanied by very different levels of anxiety in your players and that high anxiety can cause them to play badly. If one of your players is hitting first serves less than 50% of the time or is double-faulting, you might have him or her use imagery to practice serving in the following specific situations: (a) a practice session, (b) a few minutes prior to the competition, (c) when winning easily, (d) during a crucial game, or (e) with set game against them. This order represents a skills hierarchy, from the simplest situation to the most complex, that constitutes a logical learning progression. Imagery practice that incorporates hierarchical patterns may help the athlete perform better because the true-life match situations will have a familiar feel to them.

Because athletes in the advanced stage of learning know exactly how the skill should be performed, imagery can help them both see and feel themselves performing the skill. When your athletes know the feel of correct performance, imagery can be a much greater part of their total training. As the skill becomes well learned, physical practice may be de-emphasized slightly, and you can focus more on the quality of the physical practice than the quantity. Under these circumstances imagery training can be very effectively incorporated into practice.

DIFFERENT WAYS TO USE IMAGERY

Imagery techniques can be used in a variety of ways to enhance the performance of sport skills. Let's look at how it can be used to enhance skill performance, make the right decision, and improve strategy. But first, let's examine the two orientations for imagery, external and internal.

External and Internal Imagery

Imagery can have either internal or external perspective. Athletes using *internal* imagery place themselves in the actual sport situation to experience the situations and feelings they might expect to encounter during live performance. *External* imagery, in contrast, occurs when athletes view themselves from the perspective of an external observer, which is much like watching themselves on a video.

Researchers who compare the two perspectives find that internal imagery proves to be somewhat more effective; the perspective you emphasize will probably depend on the type of sport, the personality of your athlete, and the purpose of the imagery. Our advice is that you recognize the existence of both types of imagery. Some of your athletes will respond better to one of the perspectives, and one method may work better than the other for a particular skill, so be prepared to experiment to discover which form of imagery is most effective in a given situation.

Using Imagery to Enhance Performance

Imagery skills can be used to great effect immediately *preceding* the performance of a skill. Jack Nicklaus once said (Nicklaus & Bowden, 1974),

> I never hit a shot, even in practice without having a very sharp, in-focus picture of it in my head. It's like a color movie. First I "see" the ball where I want it to finish, nice and white and sitting up high on the bright green grass. Then the scene quickly changes and I "see" the ball going there; its path, trajectory, and shape, even its behavior on landing. Then there is a sort of fade-out and the next scene shows me making the kind of swing that will turn the previous images into reality. Only at the end of this short, private, Hollywood spectacular do I select a club and step up to the ball.

Consider whether your athletes might benefit from using imagery skills just prior to physical performance.

Using Imagery to Make the Correct Decision

Your athletes can use imagery to help them think through the different possibilities they might be faced with on the next play in a game. This process, known as situational decision making, enables your athletes to evaluate a specific situation and plan the next move in advance. For example, in the baseball game you are coaching, an opponent hits a ground ball to the second baseman; there are runners on first and third with one out. What should your player do? At least three options exist: The second baseman could throw to first base to get the batter out, throw to home to get the runner from third, or try turning a double play. The player's decision will depend on where the ball is hit, how quickly it is moving, how well he or she can field and throw, and so on. A second baseman who has learned to be aware of these options will respond quickly and is more likely to make the correct decision. If you are teaching imagery skills in the practice sessions, players can rehearse these options between plays and increase their chances of making the best choice.

Using Imagery to Improve Strategies of Play

Many athletes find imagery to be particularly helpful in sports in which strategy plays a significant role. Several tennis players have commented that they watch their opponents' matches and make mental notes on how they handle certain shots or respond to certain situations. They then use imagery before the game to practice hitting shots from different positions on the court to positions they had identified as weaknesses in the opponent. In addition, they visualize the strategies used by their opponents that may give them some trouble and visualize themselves taking this shot away from the opponent.

In talking to athletes in many sports, it appears that strategies are often mentally rehearsed but seldom in a systematic manner. Skilled players know, for example, where they and their opponents are, or should be, positioned at specific points in a game or match. One way to teach your athletes this skill is to have them visualize game situations and plan what they would do under various circumstances. You can show them different game situations on a blackboard, tell them the exact context of the game, and then have them use their imagery skills to look for teammates, plan the next play, and so forth.

PRINCIPLES FOR THE SUCCESSFUL USE OF IMAGERY

Imagery is a skill—a fact sometimes overlooked by coaches and athletes. You are mistaken to expect athletes to be able to use imagery techniques when you have not provided sufficient instruction and practice time. Like other skills, imagery techniques are most effectively learned through regular, well-planned practice. The following section presents ideas for beginning to develop imagery skills. For more specific advice on imagery techniques, however, refer to the ACEP Level 2 Sport Psychology Course.

Visualize Performance and Outcome

Your athletes should image both the execution of the skill and its outcome. For example, in baseball hitting, you would teach the athletes how to visualize not only the pitch but also the entire swing, the contact with the ball, the flight of the ball, and where it will end up. You should also provide the batter with the same type of real-game situations that Fred, the pitching coach described earlier in this chapter, created for his pitchers.

Pay Attention to Details

The more vivid and detailed your athletes can make their images, the better. As an example,

ice hockey players should consider the lighting, ice surface, and temperature of the rink. Moreover, the more they can concentrate on the specifics of the skill, the more they can use imagery to try out minor skill adjustments.

Feel the Skill

Tell your athletes that practice will be effective if they not only *see* themselves doing the skill but also *feel* themselves going through the motion. Developing a feel takes time, but the results are well worth the effort.

Focus on the Positive

Imagery practice should always focus on successful performance. Practicing errors will reinforce the mistake unless the practice is specifically designed to identify a particular error and correct it. If one of your athletes is having difficulty with a skill and keeps making errors, make the following suggestion and provide appropriate feedback to help correct the performance: "Image yourself making the mistake. See and feel the error." Then say, "Think about what it would take to correct the response. Image performing the skill correctly. Repeat the correct image several times. Now you try the skill."

Encourage your athletes to try this entire routine as soon after the performance as possible so that the mistake is still vivid. Do not encourage them to try this type of practice when they are emotionally upset or in a state of tension. In that condition, the athlete will probably not be very rational or objective about his or her performance.

Visualize the Entire Skill

Unless you have a specific reason for asking an athlete to concentrate on one part of a skill, all skills should be visualized in their entirety. Because skills are controlled by a motor program, it is important to practice the whole program. For example, if only the approach run to a hurdle is rehearsed, the hurdler may have problems making the transition between approaching and actually clearing the hurdle. Similar problems may be experienced in other sports if athletes fail to visualize the complete skill performance. If you should have a reason to practice parts of a skill, be sure to end your practice by rehearsing the complete skill several times.

Use Imagery Immediately Before Performance

Whenever possible, athletes should use their imagery skills to rehearse the skill at least once preceding an actual performance. Although the number and timing of rehearsals will depend on the preference of individual athletes and the limitations of their sport, you should stress that at least one mental rehearsal of the movement will be beneficial and that they should do more if they find the practice helpful.

Image Performance at Actual Speed

When mentally practicing a sport skill, the athlete should usually image the performance at its normal performance speed. Athletes have a tendency to practice a skill mentally at a much faster rate than normal performance. However, as was pointed out in Chapter 6, physical practice at performance speed is best because it enables your athletes to learn the correct timing of the skills. The same is true for mental practice.

In certain circumstances and for some of your athletes, slow-motion imagery can be a useful technique for correcting errors. You can teach them how to use slow-motion imagery to make improvements or to focus on a particularly weak part of their skill. For example, downhill skiers experiencing special difficulties with a particular stage of the course could use slow motion imagery to attempt to correct deficiencies in their technique. Once the skiers have done this successfully, however, they can and should mentally practice speeding up the skill until they can image it at performance speed.

Image for a Brief Period of Time

A limited amount of time devoted to imagery is likely to produce positive results and avoid the difficulties athletes sometimes face when they try to sustain concentration for a long time period. Many of your athletes will find that the optimal time will be perhaps only 3 to 5 minutes.

Consider the age of your athletes when teaching imagery skills. If the athletes are not able to devote complete attention to the imagery practice, they will benefit little from the exercise. Young athletes typically have a shorter attention span than adults, and they may well begin to learn bad habits if their concentration falters and they are thus visualizing incorrect technique.

WHEN TO USE IMAGERY

Practice using imagery needs no equipment, no coach, and no opposition (except in the athlete's mind), so it can be used almost anytime. Here are some examples of typical situations in which the use of imagery may enhance your athletes' performance.

During the Normal Practice Session

If one or more of your athletes are having difficulties performing a skill, it may help if you stop them and have them think through exactly what they should be doing. For example, if an athlete is having difficulty faking left before moving right, he or she might achieve greater success by stopping for a moment and imaging a fake to the left that takes the opponent off balance and allows the player to move past the opponent to the right.

Following a Successful Performance When Physical Practice Is Impossible

Golfers often mentally replay their drives when they are walking down the fairway because they cannot physically replay the shot. This technique can be effective in many other sport situations. Encourage your athletes to find a quiet place after a contest or game to think about their successful performances. Have them recall the whole performance as clearly and vividly as possible. Replaying the mental performance tape several times may help strengthen the motor program and enhance future performances.

One caution: Athletes in all sports can benefit from using imagery after successful performances; however, be sure your athletes don't begin to image when they should be paying attention to play.

When Injury Makes Physical Practice Impossible

If one of your athletes is injured and unable to participate physically in team practices or games, it is still possible for the player to use imagery to stay mentally involved in the sport. Players who stay involved with some form of participation may return to action more quickly when the injury has gone. This is one instance in which imagery can be very useful in team sports. If you are teaching new team plays, have your injured athletes run through the plays mentally. For example, if you are teaching a new offensive play and your first-string quarterback is injured, have the player image the cues the second-string quarterback is using to make the play work. This will speed up the learning process considerably. The first-string player is likely to experience suc-

cess more quickly when making the first actual attempt to execute the play.

When Trying to Overcome Boredom

Imagery has another, often unrecognized advantage. The repeated physical practice usually required to make a skill highly automated can be very boring. As athletes practice over and over again, their minds can begin to wander while their bodies go through the motions. When this occurs they will not be reinforcing the correct motor program because they are not concentrating on performing the skill correctly. In these situations athletes can develop poor habits or errors of technique. However, because imagery requires complete attention, its use can prevent your athletes from merely going through the motions. In addition, an imagery break may be just the change they need to avoid being lulled into complacency.

WHERE TO USE IMAGERY

The ideal place to hold imagery practice is the performance environment so that your athletes can become accustomed to the likely competitive conditions. The playing surface, equipment, location of spectators, weather, and many other unpredictable factors can significantly influence an athlete's performance. It is therefore vital that imagery skills be practiced whenever possible in conditions resembling actual competition to the greatest extent possible. Your athletes, however, will need to *learn* the imagery skills described in the Sport Psychology Course in a nondistracting environment first.

Of course, it is sometimes impractical to use imagery in the actual sport environment. Under those circumstances, some athletes find their imagery is enhanced by what are called *triggers*—props or objects involved in the sport—that help them concentrate on the activity. Bruce Jenner, winner of the 1976 Olympic decathlon, kept a hurdle in his living room. When asked why, he said he would mentally clear it whenever he was lying on the couch. Can you think of a way your athletes can use triggers in their imagery practice?

SUMMARY AND RECOMMENDATIONS

Imagery can be a very effective way to help your athletes learn and perform sport skills, and it becomes more and more useful as your athletes progress from the beginning to the advanced stage of learning. When using imagery have your athletes do the following:

1. Visualize both performance and outcome.
2. Pay attention to details.
3. Feel the skill.
4. Focus on the positive.
5. Image performance at actual speed.
6. Visualize the entire skill.
7. Precede physical performance with mental rehearsal.
8. Allocate 3-5 minutes to imaging the performance of a skill at any one time.
9. Supplement physical practice with imagery.
10. Use imagery during a normal practice session.
11. Use imagery following a successful performance when physical practice is impossible.
12. Use imagery when injury prevents physical practice.
13. Use imagery when inclement weather prevents physical practice.
14. Use imagery when equipment is unavailable.
15. Use imagery to overcome boredom.
16. Use imagery skills in the performance environment whenever possible.

Chapter 11
Using Memory to Retain Performance

If you have ever tried to resume playing a sport after a long period away from it, you have probably found the experience to be frustrating. You may have lost a great deal of the conditioning that was specific to performing the skills of the sport, or you may have forgotten how to execute some of the movements and perhaps even some of the plays and strategies of the game. Being unable to execute certain movements and forgetting plays are both related to *memory*. Experienced athletes can have a fairly long layoff before they start to forget either skills or plays because the skills and plays have been so well-learned. However, inexperienced athletes tend to forget much more quickly, so do not expect them to remember movements and plays from week to week very effectively, especially if you hold practices infrequently and the movements and plays are complex.

In this chapter you will learn about

- errors and memory,
- short-term memory in learning and performing skills,
- long-term memory in learning and performing skills,
- short- and long-term memory working together,
- ways to help young athletes remember.

knowledge learned at previous sessions. However, they also may have forgotten some of what you taught them last time. Their performance level may perhaps be a little lower than the level reached at the end of the previous practice session, especially if several days have elapsed between sessions. The level at which they perform will be related to how well their motor programs for the different skills have been developed—how well the skill has been learned. In addition to the loss in physical skills, they may also remember less about the rules, strategies, and teaching points they need to know to participate in the sport.

ERRORS AND MEMORY

Athletes make two distinct types of errors: errors of *movement* and errors of *knowledge*. When your athletes come to a practice session they bring with them physical skills and

Movement Errors

Because athletes can make both movement errors and knowledge errors, the distinction between what your athletes can *do* and what they *know* is important to keep in mind. It will enable you to differentiate between the two possible types of errors and put you in a better position to help your athletes make corrections. Movement errors may be caused by errors in retrieval and/or execution of a motor program. Figure 11.1 shows how this can happen. Consider this example of the four causes of movement errors. If a baseball pitcher retrieves the correct motor program for throwing a curve ball from memory and then executes it correctly, the pitch will be properly thrown (1. No cause, no movement error). However, if the pitcher retrieves the correct motor program for throwing a curve ball and then executes it incorrectly, the pitch will not be properly thrown (2. Execution error). Likewise, if the pitcher retrieves the wrong motor program and executes it either correctly (3. Retrieval error) or incorrectly (4. Retrieval and execution error), the curve ball will not be properly thrown. Errors in retrieval and/or execution of a motor program can occur in any of the three stages of skill learning but occur less often in the intermediate stages than in the beginning stage and much less often in the advanced stage than in either of the two preceding stages.

Knowledge Errors

Knowledge errors are common in sports. They occur when your athletes do not understand what you want them to do or are unable to recall what you expect of them in a particular situation. For example, while teaching tennis you may have told your players always to return the serve deep and wide into the opponent's court. If one of them is capable of placing that shot but often forgets, this is an error of knowledge. In football and soccer, athletes often make the mistake of running or passing across the field when they should be running or passing forward. In baseball, pitchers frequently forget to move toward first base when the ball is hit to that side of the infield or to backup throws to third base or home plate.

Errors and the Stages of Memory

Movement errors and knowledge errors can both be related to memory. *Memory* refers to the storage and retrieval of something that has been learned, such as sport knowledge or a motor program for a skill. As shown in Figure 11.2, memory may be divided into at least two stages: *short-term* memory and *long-term* memory.

Let's take a moment to go through the model presented in Figure 11.2. When you explain and demonstrate a new skill to your athletes, the information they receive and attend to is transmitted to their brains through the sensory system. The sensory system is capable of processing large amounts of information, but it is unable to hold it for very long—less than one second in fact. To prevent losing the information and to ensure transmitting it to short-term memory the athletes have to attend to and think about it. Once the information is transferred to short-term memory, it too will be lost, or forgotten, in a relatively short period of time—anywhere from a few seconds to several minutes—unless your athletes attend to it and physically practice the skill so that its motor program can be learned

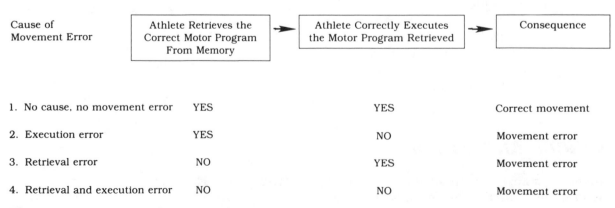

Cause of Movement Error	Athlete Retrieves the Correct Motor Program From Memory	Athlete Correctly Executes the Motor Program Retrieved	Consequence
1. No cause, no movement error	YES	YES	Correct movement
2. Execution error	YES	NO	Movement error
3. Retrieval error	NO	YES	Movement error
4. Retrieval and execution error	NO	NO	Movement error

Figure 11.1 Four possible causes of movement errors.

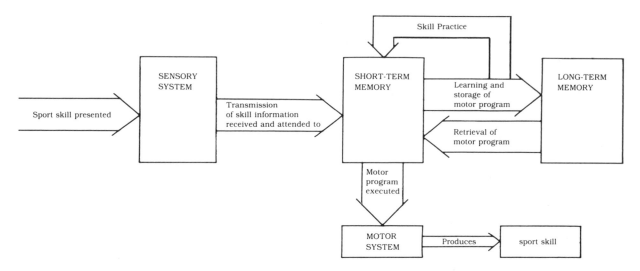

Figure 11.2   Model of the stages of memory involved in performing a sport skill.

and stored in long-term memory. The more highly practiced and well learned the motor program for a skill, the more permanently stored it is in long-term memory and the more resistant it is to being forgotten. Long-term memory has a virtually unlimited capacity for storing information such as sport knowledge or motor programs, whereas short-term memory's capacity is very limited. As you can see in Figure 11.2, when your athletes need to retrieve the motor program for a skill from long-term memory, they do so by using short-term memory as a temporary working memory from which to launch performance. It is here that the retrieval errors we discussed earlier can be made. Once the motor program is retrieved, it is executed by the motor system. This is where the execution errors can occur. The sport skill is being produced while the motor system executes the motor program.

SHORT-TERM MEMORY IN LEARNING AND PERFORMING SKILLS

If you give your athletes a great deal of information, many of them will be unable to remember all the details. A common coaching error is to talk far too long about how to perform a skill before letting the athletes try the skill for themselves. These coaches fail to appreciate that long lectures are an ineffective

form of instruction. We all tend to forget information unless we make a conscious effort to learn and retain it in memory, and this is especially true of young athletes. You need to teach them to make a conscious effort to *attend to* what you are teaching as well as to *rehearse* the material. Attention means consciously watching or listening to whomever is talking or demonstrating without being distracted; rehearsing refers to repeating information to oneself.

Your own short-term memory is tested every time you begin coaching a new group of athletes. For example, how successfully can you remember each athlete's name? How quickly you get to know their names significantly influences how your athletes feel about themselves and about you. Moreover, your athletes will learn skills faster if you teach them techniques to help them remember most of what they learned at the previous practice session.

Information must become part of long-term memory if your athletes are to remember movements and knowledge for as long as possible. Remember, short-term memory lasts only a few seconds to a few minutes. The transfer to long-term memory is best achieved if you routinely (a) emphasize key learning points during your skill explanations and demonstrations and (b) allow plenty of time for physical practice. One effective instructional technique is always to start and end your explanations by emphasizing the key learning points. Also consider how you can communicate most effectively. You can help your athletes retain knowledge by using verbal labels (discussed in chapter 3) or simple analogies. For example, teach your athletes that the backswing of the tennis serve is very similar to the action of scratching one's back; they will be much more likely to remember this description than an explanation of movement mechanics. No matter how effectively you communicate information and how well your athletes remember instructions, without physical practice they may have difficulty remembering how to perform the skill. If you explained how to snowplow to a group of beginning skiers but let them have only one practice, they might remember your instructions but will probably have forgotten or lost the feel of the skill by the next session.

Repetition and Rehearsal

Repetition and rehearsal will greatly enhance your athletes' memories. For example, following a skill explanation you might select an athlete to repeat what you just said (this step also keeps *all* the athletes attending if they are uncertain who will be asked to provide an explanation). This same strategy can be extended to provide rehearsal. Ask an athlete to explain in his or her own words how a skill is performed. Presenting the explanation will make the athlete mentally review or rehearse each of the steps involved.

Repetition and rehearsal are also helpful in retaining knowledge. When first trying to learn each other's names (knowledge), for example, you might tell each athlete to introduce him- or herself and then tell the other athletes to repeat this person's name several times. If you follow the same procedure, both you and your athletes will learn the names more quickly. Another strategy is to get each athlete to tell the team a little about him- or herself. This will force the athletes to rehearse each other's names and, at the same time, enable them to associate something about the athlete with the name.

Practice and Competition

When athletes perform skills in either practice or competition, they are frequently *thinking* about the game (i.e., what are the strengths of the opposition?) and also *deciding* how to react to their opponents. Thinking about what is happening and deciding what to do are both highly dependent on short-term memory. Short-term memory is used during competitive situations when we tell athletes what to think about at specific points in a game. In basketball, for example, if an opposing player has four personal fouls, he or she will be unable to play aggressively. We would want to be sure that all players on our team were aware of the situation and were prepared to exploit it. However, this kind of specific information need be remembered only for the duration of the game because it is unimportant once the game is over.

Short-term memory is also used during competition for decision making and for planning strategy. When a skilled soccer goalkeeper defends against a shot, he or she is aware of not only where all the opposing players are, but is also thinking about whom to pass to after making the save. These strategy decisions are retained in short-term memory.

Athletes can respond much more quickly to events if they are expecting them and have used short-term memory to help prepare their response. This is why in football it is much easier to blitz on an offense that often runs the same type of play in certain situations. For example, if a team always passes deep on the third down when 7 to 10 yards are needed, the player or players blitzing know from past experience who will be blocking against them and will be able to plan ways to contain the blocker and get the quarterback. In chapter 13 we will discuss additional ways to help your athletes react more quickly.

LONG-TERM MEMORY IN LEARNING AND PERFORMING SKILLS

Information you or your athletes remember from practice to practice has been stored in long-term memory. As athletes move from the beginning learning stage through to the advanced stage, more and more information moves from short-term to long-term memory. Sometimes, however, even highly skilled athletes perform skills in a manner suggesting that they have forgotten either how to make the movement or when to execute it. How can this occurrence be explained? Consider, for example, the skilled golfer who has played so regularly that it is evident the player has formulated and stored a motor program in long-term memory. Following an injury that keeps the golfer out of action for 3 months, the player discovers that he or she is no longer able to putt well. The skill, or parts of it, appear to have been forgotten. Forgetting can take place for one of two reasons: (a) the passage of time in which no practice took place or (b) interference of other activities with what has already been learned and stored in long-term memory.

Passage of Time

Too long a time between practice sessions is one reason for forgetting. If athletes do not practice frequently enough, they may forget what you want them to do or how you want them to do it. This form of forgetting is especially critical when skills have a *high cognitive element*, as, for example, the golf putting action. It's easy for golfers to forget all of the details of the stance needed to putt successfully. Similar problems frequently arise when performing other fine motor skills in which a precise position is needed; for example, shooting and archery. If you have athletes who have not performed a skill for several months or perhaps since the previous season, do not be surprised if some of them need to relearn some skills.

Interference

Another reason for forgetting how to perform a previously learned skill is that other learned movements either interfere with retrieval of the motor program from long-term memory or actually weaken the stored motor program. If you notice a change or deterioration in an athlete's technique, you should find out if the individual is practicing a similar skill at the same time. For example, practicing the golf swing during the baseball season can be detrimental to the effectiveness of the baseball swing. Some athletes have found that field hockey has a negative effect on golf and that badminton adversely influences tennis. As

you learned in chapter 7, the extent of the interference depends on the relationship between the different skills.

SHORT- AND LONG-TERM MEMORY WORKING TOGETHER

In competitive sport situations short-term and long-term memory interact in a cooperative way. Consider the following ice hockey example. The player is streaking down the ice and attempting to score on a breakaway. The player intently watches the goalkeeper while stick handling into position for a shot on goal, and his or her eyes register the opponent's position and transmit the information into short-term memory. The position data may then be combined with information in long-term memory about how that player normally responds to breakaways. Is the goalkeeper weaker to the right or left side? Does he or she normally rush opponents? Is he or she better at defending high or low shots? The offensive player must interpret this combined information and decide whether to shoot from a distance or move in closer, possibly skating around the goalkeeper. A shot is selected, and—if the retrieval process is successful—the appropriate motor program executes the attempt to score. Consider how this process might actually operate: The attacker sees that the goalkeeper's stick is down low; he or she is starting to move out to confront the skater, who chooses to shoot early and high to the top of the net.

Although athletes are not able to exercise complete control over the interaction between short-term and long-term memory, they can be taught to focus on certain aspects of performance and to ignore others. The ability of your athletes to change the focus of attention becomes especially important when they remember parts of a performance that might adversely affect future performances. For example, if your football team has just finished a preseason game in wet and cold conditions and made many mistakes, you might remind them that the conditions were bad, such performances are to be expected, and that they should forget the performance and concentrate on the next game. In the *Coaches Guide to Sport Psychology* (Martens, 1987), various techniques are explained to help you redirect your athletes' attention from those aspects of previous performances that are presently creating performance problems.

WAYS TO HELP YOUNG ATHLETES REMEMBER

If you coach younger children you should understand that their memories function in ways that are significantly different from that of adults. In remembering, children—as opposed to adults—use inefficient strategies to store information in memory (Thomas, Thomas, & Gallagher, 1984). You therefore need to help them organize and develop useful strategies for organizing and retaining information in memory.

As with adults, information arrives in short-term memory through the eyes, ears, and other sensory organs. Short-term memory is thus called upon when using this information to make decisions and retrieve motor programs. As a coach, you can help young athletes improve their ability to use their short-term memories effectively when learning and performing skills by helping them to

• rehearse and repeat what they see, hear, and practice,

• group and recode information to enhance memory, and

• broaden their movement experience.

Rehearsal and Repetition

Young athletes need help when learning how to retain information in memory. As we noted earlier in this chapter, rehearsal or practice is a key to improving sport performance. For example, in football a young pass receiver must have some way to know how to run a 12-yard square out. The yardage lines are not reliable because a play can start anywhere on the field. Adults will know that they can count steps, but children need to be taught this skill. Similarly, young swimmers need to be taught how to count arm strokes to know when to turn when swimming the backstroke. Unless skills are extremely complex, simply telling young athletes to repeat important pieces of information or having them rehearse the skill over and over is often enough to help them remember it.

Group and Recode Information to Enhance Memory

If you were asked to look at the following chart for 5 seconds, then close the book and try to write out the chart, could you do it?

```
A T H
L E T
E S F
I R S
T WI
N N I
N G S
E C O
N D
```

When adults are given too much information to remember, they know that the task can be simplified by regrouping the information in a way that is easy to remember. The list of abstract letters shown above is quite easy to remember when grouped into the words ATHLETES FIRST WINNING SECOND. However, whereas information is often automatically recoded by adults, children may not recode information automatically. When you coach you should always think about the best way you can group and organize information for easy storage in memory. Using short, clear teaching points and verbal labels in your skill explanations is probably the most effective way of achieving this goal.

Broaden Athletes' Movement Experiences

Because adults have greater movement experience than children, they have a better understanding of the various movement options available and can perform many more movements with little or no practice. For example, you could tell an adult athlete to hop, hop, skip, skip, and jump. Most athletes would remember this sequence of five instructions and be able to carry it out without much practice. In contrast, most young children would both forget the instructions and, even if they remembered them, not have the movement experience to execute the hops, skips, and jump.

Try to include a great variety of movement experiences into your practices when coaching young athletes. If exposed to many different movements, athletes will later find it much easier to integrate these movement experiences into the performance of the younger athlete's memory. Break movement sequences into small parts and be sure they have learned one sequence before progressing to the next. The recommendations that follow suggest additional ideas for helping your young athletes remember.

SUMMARY AND RECOMMENDATIONS

The ability to learn and to perform sport skills and to remember plays and strategy is in-

fluenced by memory. The errors that athletes make are either (a) errors of movement or (b) errors of knowledge. To be able to make the appropriate corrections, coaches must learn to distinguish between these different types of errors. In addition, strategies must be adopted that will enhance athletes' short-term and long-term memories. The following recommendations illustrate the various ways in which you can help your athletes to remember skills and knowledge and thereby improve their learning.

1. Emphasize key learning points through clear and concise explanations and demonstrations.
2. Start and end all explanations with key learning points.
3. Relate new skills to previously learned skills.
4. Break skills into smaller parts using combinations of whole and part practice methods.
5. Make skills meaningful by showing their importance and thereby increasing your athletes' motivation.
6. Use simple playing systems and plan alternatives using verbal labels and verbal pretraining.
7. Use imagery to practice skills between sessions.
8. Give the athletes supplementary information (e.g., pictures and handouts) to pin up at home.
9. Overpractice skills by continuing to practice learned skills.
10. Practice skills under fatigued conditions if they must be performed when athletes are fatigued.
11. Do not leave too much time between practice sessions in order to prevent forgetting.

Chapter 12

Attention and Variables Influencing Its Focus

Any time you want your athletes to listen to you or watch a demonstration, you need their attention; otherwise, they will not learn the skill you are trying to teach. Remember, information is stored in memory when it is attended to; merely noticing that an explanation or demonstration is occurring will not enhance learning.

Two terms require clarification when we discuss attention: perception and attention. Both are highly related, with perception being the starting point for attention.

Perception is the process by which we become aware of events in the environment and interpret their significance. Once you have perceived an event, you are then left with the question of deciding whether or not to continue to pay attention to it and how to react to it.

Attention is the mechanism by which we become involved in events in the environment. One way to think of paying attention is to imagine focusing a beam of light on an object in a dark room. We see the object when the beam falls on it. Similarly, when we attend to any of the multitude of stimuli impinging on our senses, we first perceive them and then process them for storage in memory. For example, an athlete might perceive movement to his or her right and then attend to that movement. By so doing, the athlete can make appropriate decisions based on the events, provided that he or she has learned an appropriate response or strategy. Such decision making would be impossible without attention.

Several factors influence your athletes' ability to pay attention. These factors are the focus of this chapter. You will learn about the following topics:

- Arousal and attention
- The senses and attention
- Factors influencing selective attention
- Helping your athletes focus attention

AROUSAL AND ATTENTION

All athletes need to exert control over how psyched up they become when performing sport skills because when athletes have high levels of arousal, their ability to attend to appropriate cues changes. For example, as your athletes' arousal level changes, their ability to be aware of many events occurring simultaneously changes. At a very simple level, an inverted U shape, shown in Figure 12.1, characterizes the optimal arousal level for performance.

The information in the figure suggests that optimal performance occurs at moderate levels of arousal. However, so simple an explanation fails to consider at least four factors that affect the optimum level of arousal for your athletes. These factors include

- the type of sport you are teaching,
- differences in position,
- the skill level of your athletes, and
- individual differences.

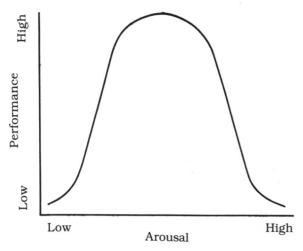

Figure 12.1 The relationship between arousal and performance resembles an inverted *U*.

What Sport Skill Are You Teaching?

The optimal arousal level for learning or performing sport skills depends on whether the skills are (a) fine or gross and (b) open or closed. The classification of fine versus gross skills depends on the types of muscles being used and how precisely they need to be controlled.

Fine Versus Gross Skills

Fine motor skills are those requiring movement of smaller, less powerful muscle groups and involve little movement. They generally require accuracy more than strenuous activity, for example, writing your name on a small piece of paper. *Gross motor skills*, however, require greater expenditures of physical effort and are characterized by large movements and large muscle involvement. Writing your name on a chalkboard so that it is 3 feet high and 8 feet in length is an example of a gross motor skill.

All sport skills fall on a continuum between fine and gross motor skills. At one end of the continuum are fine sport skills such as rifle shooting and putting in golf; at the other end are gross skills like weight lifting and blocking and tackling in football.

Compare the skill of putting in golf with weight lifting. In putting, athletes must exert precise control over their arm muscles. Optimal performance requires that the athlete is relaxed and at a relatively low level of arousal. In contrast, in weight lifting the entire muscular system must be highly aroused. Optimum arousal levels for these and other sport skills are shown in Figure 12.2.

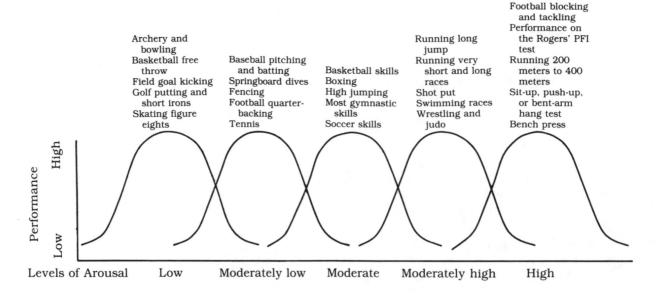

Figure 12.2 Optimum arousal levels for peak performance for different types of sport skills. From "Emotional Arousal and Motor Performance" by J.B. Oxendine, 1970, *Quest, XIII*, pp. 23-32. Copyright 1970 by Quest Board. Modified by permission.

Open Versus Closed Skills

Skills can be classified according to the extent to which the environment is predictable during the performance. As can be seen in Figure 12.3, the environment is largely predictable for closed skills, whereas in open skills the environment is changing and unpredictable. One affect of arousal is that it narrows the visual field of the athlete; in other words, it makes it more difficult to attend to all of the relevant stimuli.

In many open-skill sports it is especially important to have a broad visual field. If we consider all the options a quarterback must consider, it is obvious he needs a very broad focus of attention to pick up all his receivers as well as the defensive coverage. Athletes whose performance is dependent on their awareness of what is happening around them must stay at medium levels of arousal.

Closed skills tend to have fewer relevant cues because the environment doesn't change. As a result, those skills are less severely affected by narrowing of the visual field. However, if arousal causes an athlete's visual field to narrow too much, the athlete could miss a relevant cue for a closed skill.

Think about the type of skills required in the sport you coach. What type of skills are they? What is the optimum level of arousal for each of your athletes?

Differences in Position

Even within the same sport, the optimal level of arousal appropriate for playing different positions is variable. For example, compare the performance of a quarterback making a 20-yard pass with that of a blitzing linebacker. As indicated in Figure 12.2, the quarterback needs to be at a medium level of arousal, needs to be sufficiently aroused to run, throw, and withstand being tackled, but must also be aware of everything that is happening on the field of play to read the defense and select a receiver. An overaroused quarterback may fail to notice a receiver free for a pass due to a narrowing of the visual field. This is just like looking for several objects at once in a dark room with a narrowly focused flashlight. You have to scan. Using this strategy, you are likely to miss important cues.

To get a feel for this narrowing and scanning, roll a piece of paper into a tubular shape. Now try to observe what is going on around you solely by looking through the tube. Did you continually shift your visual field? Did you feel that you were less in touch with your surroundings? That is the essential effect on the overaroused quarterback. As a result, appropriate cues will remain unattended.

Unlike the quarterback, a linebacker has only one task to perform. If he has been told to blitz the quarterback, his optimal level of arousal is high, which gives him the strength and speed to break through the offensive line and sack the quarterback. He does not have to worry about what else might be happening on the field. If underaroused, the linebacker may be unable to break through the offensive line. Even for a linebacker, though, overarousal remains a possibility, and regardless of the sport, overarousal will impede performance. The linebacker needs to be sufficiently calm to spot the easiest way through the line.

Closed skills
(Environment predominantly predictable)

Open skills
(Environment predominantly unpredictable)

Golf swing
Discus throw
Handstand
Platform dive

- Guarding an offensive player who has many moves in basketball
- Returning a kickoff in football
- Defending against shots taken on goal in hockey
- Hitting a knuckleball in baseball

Figure 12.3 A continuum of open and closed skills in sport.

How Skilled Are Your Athletes?

When teaching beginners, you should take care to create a relaxed atmosphere in which the athletes can concentrate on learning the skill. Use a calm, quiet tone of voice and make sure the athletes do not feel threatened. With advanced performers who have well-developed motor programs, you may need to motivate them (in a positive way) to learn new skills or refine previously learned skills. You might expect, additionally, your more skilled athletes to have greater ability to control their arousal. This control will help them perform more efficiently and effectively than beginners.

Individual Differences

All athletes need to be treated as individuals. Some athletes learn and perform best when highly aroused, whereas others perform better at much lower levels of arousal. Get to know each of your athletes and how they respond to different situations. If an athlete is often anxious, use a low-key approach when teaching a skill. Conversely, other athletes may respond to a more upbeat approach. Various ways to help your athletes manipulate their arousal level are discussed in the *Coaches Guide to Sport Psychology* (Martens, 1987).

THE SENSES AND ATTENTION

In addition to arousal level, attention is influenced by senses such as sight, sound, and feel. Even if you have taught your athletes to identify and attend to the appropriate cues, you must make sure that their sensory organs (e.g., eyes and ears) are functioning optimally so that they can interpret the cues efficiently and correctly. Determine which senses are important in your sport.

Next, you need to decide which abilities within that sense are vital. For example, according to Landers & Daniels (1983), world-class rifle shooters possess *distance* acuity of 20/20 and pistol shooters have a *near* acuity of 20/20. The rifle shooter must have sharp vision at the target whereas the pistol shooter must see the front sight clearly.

Vision

The sport you coach undoubtedly makes some special demands on your athletes' vision. You should become aware of which abilities are important for your sport.

The American Optometric Association (n.d.) had reported that one out of five athletes has sight defects that, if uncorrected, could adversely affect performance. Vision is usually measured according to the following characteristics.

- *Distant acuity*: The ability to focus on and make out fine detail at 20 feet or more with each eye separately and together under a variety of lighting conditions is beneficial to maximize an athlete's potential in most sports.
- *Nearpoint vision*: The ability to focus and see clearly close up is also important. Athletes must often rapidly change focus from a distant object to a near object.
- *Depth perception*: The ability to be able to judge speed and distance relationships quickly and accurately is vital in virtually every sport activity.
- *Dynamic visual acuity*: The ability of the observer to detect details of an object when there is movement between the observer and the object is necessary in many sports. Examples might include football, volleyball, and other sports involving moving objects.

- *Field of vision*: The amount of area that can be seen without moving the eyes or head is quite important. Athletes in most sports need a wide field of vision on both sides and up and down. This ability eliminates unnecessary head and eye movement.
- *Binocular coordination*: Your athletes must have both their eyes functioning together in a precise manner.
- *Good color vision*: Your athletes must be able to identify different colors and hues. Below-normal color vision can often be compensated for. For example, choose a team uniform that is so distinctive that it can be recognized without reference to color.
- *Glare recovery*: You must make sure that your athletes can perform well in a variety of different lighting situations.

All of these characteristics can be tested for and corrected by an optometrist but are seldom checked during a routine visit. Consider suggesting to your athletes that they be checked for all aspects of vision that apply to their particular sport. If any of your athletes is having difficulty learning and performing skills, have his or her vision checked. In some sports this will be more important than in others—especially those in which following small, moving objects are involved; for example, racquet sports, shooting sports, and archery.

Hearing

Have you ever called out advice to an athlete and then watched in dismay as the advice was not heeded or the skill was executed incorrectly? One possible explanation for this occurrence is that the athlete did not hear your advice or misheard what you suggested. Hearing is an extremely important sense in many sports. When communicating tactics, you may not be heard clearly because of the amount of noise during a game. In these instances, you must plan alternative forms of communication, such as hand and eye signals. In tennis, players can learn to identify the type of shot their opponents have made by listening carefully. To the attentive ear, spins and slices each have a distinctive sound. Can you think of ways that sound might affect your athletes' performance?

Kinesthesis

Do you remember performing a skill that felt just right? Many highly skilled athletes have a well-developed sense of how a movement should feel. Unfortunately, we know very little about how to teach athletes to develop their kinesthetic sense. Our best advice is to experiment with different approaches with your athletes. Some athletes may respond to a teaching approach in which you emphasize the *feel* of the skill. One way to implement such an approach is to limit the other senses so that the athletes must rely on their kinesthetic sense— the feel of the movement. As an example, you can follow this approach quite easily in wrestling. Have your athletes wrestle blindfolded or with their eyes closed. You'll be amazed at how much they learn to identify with the feel of their movements and those of the opponent.

Gallwey (1974) made some useful suggestions for heightening kinesthetic awareness in tennis players that can easily be generalized to all sports. He suggests that tennis players may benefit from undergoing some sensitivity training with their bodies, which can be accomplished by focusing their attention on their bodies during practice. Ideally, a teammate or ball machine would throw balls that bounce in approximately the same spot each time to the tennis player. Then, paying relatively little attention to the ball, the players can experience what it feels like to hit the ball. One aspect to concentrate on is feeling the exact path of the racquet on the backswing. However, attention should be mainly focused on the feel of the arm and hand at the moment just before they swing forward to meet the ball.

Many of you will be aware of the problems with this kind of approach. Beginners will be unable to identify the feel of a movement because they have nothing with which to compare it. On the opposite end of the performance continuum, highly skilled players might suffer from what has been termed *paralysis from analysis*. Knowing when to emphasize the feel of a skill and with which athletes to try this approach is a prime example of why coaching is an art as well as a science. As we suggested at the beginning of this chapter, experiment with different approaches for each of your athletes, then stick with the method that is most effective for the individuals with whom you work.

FACTORS INFLUENCING SELECTIVE ATTENTION

In addition to helping your athletes control their level of arousal and making sure they can perceive stimuli, you can also help them improve their performance by teaching them to attend to the most important stimuli by improving their selective attention skills. Selective attention refers to the ability to focus on, or to attend to, a limited number of events happening in a game or contest. To help your athletes attend to the most important cues, you need to be aware that selective attention is influenced by several factors, some external and others internal. We will discuss one external factor and three internal factors that affect your athletes' ability to pay attention.

Orienting Response

The orienting response, an external factor, alerts people to anything out of the ordinary in the environment. Any time something unexpected happens, we start to pay attention without consciously thinking about it. Several characteristics influence how we respond to an event, including its intensity, size, shape, novelty, contrast with the surrounding environment, and the manner in which it moves.

As coaches, you have often taken advantage of this response by suddenly blowing a whistle or doing anything that takes your athletes by surprise. However, this response usually needs to be overridden in sports. Consider what would happen if, instead of maintaining attention on the sport, your athletes were always distracted by noises in the crowd. If your athletes are easily distracted by unexpected events, you should consider teaching them concentration skills as described in the *Coaches Guide to Sport Psychology* (Martens, 1987).

Interest

It is very hard to pay attention to something boring. Conversely, athletes readily attend to activities in which they are interested. You should therefore make special efforts to keep your practice sessions interesting and challenging. But this is much easier in some sports than others. In coaching tennis, for example, you can devise many varied drills and activities to challenge your athletes continuously. Swimming is somewhat more difficult; nevertheless, use your imagination. You can help keep interest high by frequently changing drills or the focus of attention. A word of caution—you still need to spend the needed time practicing. Avoid the shotgun approach, which is fun and uses many different activities but accomplishes little.

Mind Set

Selective attention can be greatly influenced by the mind set of your athletes. Whenever you give your athletes cues upon which to focus, you are helping them improve their selective attention skills. Attending to the cues you have identified will help your athletes learn new skills by reducing the number of cues for attention and eliminating devoting attention to irrelevant cues.

Having a cue-related mind set also helps athletes perform better. Because many sports require athletes to make decisions in a very short period of time, identifying cues that will enable athletes to respond quickly can be a major advantage. You will read more about the importance of teaching your athletes to anticipate and respond quickly in chapter 13.

Ability to Screen Information

Some athletes are much better than others at filtering out irrelevant information in the environment and can be described as screeners. These athletes have the ability to focus on the relevant cues in the environment. Nonscreeners, on the other hand, tend to focus attention diffusely and have trouble in both selecting appropriate stimuli and shifting attention (Mehrabian, 1976). You should try to identify athletes who have problems focusing and shifting attention; help them overcome this limitation. Additional information is provided in the *Coaches Guide to Sport Psychology* (Martens, 1987).

HELPING YOUR ATHLETES FOCUS ATTENTION

Athletes need to be taught which parts of their game and which parts of the opponent's game require their concentration. If you teach your athletes to attend to very specific aspects of the sporting environment, they will be able to detect the most important cues more easily. Although the types of cues will differ from sport to sport, two general guidelines can be recommended: focusing on a small number of cues and selecting meaningful cues.

Focus on a Small Number of Cues

Athletes are able to pay attention to a limited number of events at a time. The greatest difficulty, especially for beginning athletes, is knowing where to focus when so much seems to be happening around them. You need to provide one or two simple cues to help them. For example, in most team sports there are key playing principles to guide the actions of offensive and defensive players. Principles or strategies simplify complex situations and provide athletes with guidelines for action. When you are coaching, always try to give each individual athlete a small number of relevant cues to guide his or her actions.

Select Meaningful Cues

It is important to develop your athletes' ability to focus their attention on only a small number of events, but it is even more critical that they learn to focus on the *most important cues* that will enhance learning and performance. They need to identify the skills and cues in the game that need their concentration. Likewise they need to know which cues they should ignore.

If you teach your athletes to attend to very specific aspects of the sporting environment, they will be able to detect the most important cues from teammates and from the opposition. For example, one easy way to dribble past a player in soccer is to use a body feint. Some players are very good at using their arms or their shoulders to send defenders the wrong

way. Players who have not been taught what to attend to will often watch the opponent's body and find themselves going the wrong way. Players always go where their feet take them, so a skilled coach would tell the players to concentrate solely on watching the opponent's feet and not to allow themselves to be distracted by any arm or head fakes.

Football is another sport in which the ability to identify cues is important. If you are coaching the defensive line, you might tell your athletes to watch the offensive lineman's eyes to see if he is looking at the player he is going to block. Alternatively, by watching the way he is leaning, you often will see that he is "cheating" toward the person he is going to block.

Make sure that your athletes find your suggested cues meaningful. What is meaningful to the coach may be impractical or unrealistic for an athlete's use. High-board divers, for instance, need to be told the cues that are useful to maintain the correct orientation and body position while twisting and rotating. Nideffer (1985) relates a conversation with Ron O'Brien, the coach of the 1984 U.S. Olympic Diving Team, about spotting dives. Some divers have problems spotting the tower, but two-time Olympic Champion Greg Louganis has the ability to read a sign with a five-digit number on it, an ability few other divers have developed. Individual differences between athletes will affect your selection of appropriate cues for them to attend to.

Look for cues that will be meaningful for the greatest number of athletes. In baseball, for example, a pitcher will sometimes use a slightly different wind-up to throw a curveball than a fastball. Perhaps the wrist is flexed more before the delivery of the curve. This can often be seen by looking above the pitcher's shoulder at the point from which the ball is delivered or by noticing whether the pitcher has a higher leg kick with a fastball. Teach your batters to be alert to both of these cues, and they will all know what type of pitch is about to be thrown. This kind of knowledge will help them anticipate more effectively—the subject of the next chapter.

Like general playing principles and strategies, general teaching cues should be learned by all your athletes, and they must also be meaningful to the athletes. Select cues that are meaningful to a group of athletes but be sensitive, as well, to the need to individualize cues.

SUMMARY AND RECOMMENDATIONS

The ability to pay attention to relevant cues while performing sport skills is affected by arousal level. By controlling arousal levels athletes can attend to the appropriate cues more efficiently. However, the optimal arousal level for each skill varies according to the type of skill involved and individual variation among athletes. The following recommendations outline some of the practice steps you can take to improve the ability of your athletes to pay attention.

1. Manipulate the arousal level of your athletes based on the type of skill (fine vs. gross, open vs. closed), the position, the skill level of the athlete, and how each individual responds to different states of arousal.

2. Consider a vision check if any of your athletes are experiencing difficulties learning skills in which good vision is required.
3. Check that your instructions can be clearly heard by all athletes.
4. When teaching new skills or correcting errors, consider ways of changing the focus of your athletes' attention away from the *mechanics* of the movement toward developing a *feel* for the movement. Remember, too much attention on mechanics of the skill can lead to paralysis from analysis.
5. Improve the ability of your athletes to selectively attend to the most important information in the learning environment by teaching them how to

   • focus on a small number of cues and
   • select meaningful cues.

Chapter 13
Anticipation and Learning to Respond Quickly

The best sprinters in track and the best short-distance racers in swimming are able to get off the blocks so quickly—how do they do it? Why are the best defensive players in basketball able to respond so quickly to their opponents' maneuvers? Why do the best soccer and hockey goalkeepers appear to make so many split-second saves? Although many people believe the answer is lightning-fast reflexes, the ability to respond quickly, contrary to popular opinion, has little to do with reflexes. Reflexes are involuntary, innate responses to stimuli involved in such actions as maintaining upright posture, regulating respiration and cardiovascular functions, withdrawing from painful stimuli, and controlling locomotion.

The simplest and perhaps best-known example of a reflex is the knee-jerk reflex (a stretch reflex), often demonstrated by having a person sit on a table with his or her legs bent at the knees with the lower legs hanging straight down but not touching the floor. The patellar tendon located just below the kneecap (patella) of one of the legs is tapped (stimulus), and after a brief delay the lower leg automatically starts to swing forward and upward (response). Unlike the movements that make up sport skills, reflexes are unlearned. The neural circuits for reflexes are present at birth or develop automatically during the early years of life.

Although reflexes are involved to some extent in the actions we make in various sport situations, they are not chiefly responsible for athletes' ability to make quick, voluntary responses to stimuli. The real key to responding quickly is being able to react and move quickly—both of which are influenced by a number of factors. If fast voluntary responses are important in your sport, understanding

how they take place and the factors influencing them is vital. Knowing the mechanisms and situational factors affecting response time will enable you to teach your athletes how to overcome performance limitations imposed by slow reactions and/or slow movements. You can also help them learn to respond a little bit quicker in important situations. In this chapter you will learn about

- the components of response time,
- ways to overcome slow responses,
- factors influencing reaction time, and
- helping your athletes to anticipate.

THE COMPONENTS OF RESPONSE TIME

To understand the terms *reaction time, movement time* and *response time*, consider how a tennis player functions in response to an opponent's shot. The diagram in Figure 13.1 depicts the processes that must occur to allow returning the tennis ball with a forehand stroke. Notice that the time it takes for the player to respond depends on the combination of reaction time and movement time, which, taken together, make up response time. Specifically, the foreperiod is the time from the opponent's action, which provides a cue indicating that the player should get ready to return the shot using a forehand stroke, until the instant when flight of the ball acts as a stimulus to begin the stroke. The *reaction time* is the time from when the flight of the approaching ball acts as a stimulus to begin the forehand stroke until the player initiates the

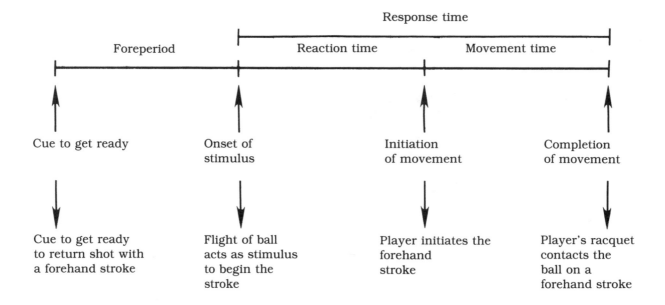

Figure 13.1 The components of response time.

stroke. The time from the initiation of the forehand stroke until its completion, when the racquet contacts the ball, is the *movement time*. Finally, the time from the onset of the stimulus to begin the forehand stroke until the racquet contacts the ball is the *response time*. In other words, reaction time plus movement time equals response time.

Individual differences in your athletes' abilities to react fast and to move fast are almost completely unrelated. Your athletes with fast reaction times may or may not have fast movement times. Thus attempting to predict the speed of one based on the speed of the other is usually unsuccessful.

WAYS TO OVERCOME SLOW RESPONSES

The reaction time of individuals varies, but for the player in Figure 13.1, let's say it takes about 200 milliseconds (2/10 of a second) to react to the visual stimulus—the flight of the approaching tennis ball. After a player has initiated the stroke, he or she still has to complete it, which could take another 200 milliseconds. As a result, the time from when a tennis player sees how to hit the ball to when the racquet actually makes contact totals about 400 milliseconds (4/10 of a second). An interval of 400 milliseconds leaves little time for a player to react and move in response to a stimulus.

Consider, for example, a fast serve from a female tennis player on the Penn State University team. The average speed of her serve is 91 miles per hour. Because the distance the ball travels is at least 60 feet, it takes the ball 450 milliseconds to reach the player if she is standing close to the service line. Therefore, if the player returning the serve has a response time of 400 milliseconds, she has to start making her move about 50 milliseconds after the ball has left the racquet of the server, when the ball is still in the backcourt of her opponent. Three possible strategies the player might use to return the serve are described in the following sections. Consider how these strategies or combinations of them might help your athletes overcome response-time delays due to reacting and/or moving too slowly.

Shorten the Distance of the Movement

Suppose the tennis player does not have time to use a full backswing when returning a fast serve. One way to give her more time is to teach her how to reduce the movement distance of her backswing. If she shortens the backswing, the movement time will also be reduced if the average velocity is held constant. The same principle applies to other sport situations in which athletes must strike fast-moving objects, such as a high-velocity baseball or softball pitch that requires the batter to use a half swing to get the bat around in time to hit the ball.

Move Faster

The tennis player's total response time depends on the combination of her reaction time and movement time, so one obvious way to decrease movement time is to move faster. As an alternative to the suggestion made to reduce the backswing movement, have this player try to maintain the full backswing but swing faster than normal when attempting a fast return of the high-speed serve. Of course, although athletes who can swing fast or move fast are able to respond faster than average, fast movements are often gained at the expense of accuracy, as you learned in chapter 6.

The faster a movement is made, the more difficult it is to maintain accuracy (Fitts, 1954). In Figure 13.2 you will see three pairs of circular targets. Holding a pencil as you do when you write but without touching your hand or arm to the desk top, place the tip of the pencil on one of the two targets opposite *very slow speed*. Now lift the pencil and move it very slowly and as accurately as possible from one target to the other target, back and forth for 10 seconds. Count the number of times your pencil accurately hits and misses each target. If you moved slowly enough, you should have hit the targets either all the time or at least many more times than you missed them. Now try it again, this time moving faster while trying to hit the targets opposite *moderate speed*. You should find that you make a greater number of movements, but you also miss the targets more often. Now try the exercise moving as fast as possible while trying to hit the targets opposite *very fast speed*. You should find

that you make the greatest number of movements at this speed, but you also miss the targets more often than at the slower speed. This exercise demonstrates the speed-accuracy tradeoff. Increasing the speed of your movements decreased their accuracy, and increasing the accuracy of your movements decreases their speed. Many athletes face exactly the same dilemma in their chosen sports; for example, baseball and softball batters. The faster they swing, the more difficulty they have hitting a well-pitched ball, and the slower they swing, the easier it is to hit it.

This speed-accuracy tradeoff is evident in many sport situations and is often responsible for the performance errors we observe. The basketball player hurries the shot, shoots too quickly, and sees the ball miss the basket; the tennis player hits a blistering return only to watch it land out of court; the gymnast moves so fast that he or she cannot get enough height to complete the double somersault; and the pitcher throws the baseball so fast that it does not find the strike zone. In each of these situations the athlete failed to reach an efficient compromise between speed of movement and accuracy of movement. Learning the correct balance between speed and accuracy in sport skills is a challenge for all athletes. If you notice that one of your athletes is experiencing difficulty in performing accurate movements, consider whether an excessive emphasis on speed might be the root of the problem. If so, advise the athlete to slow down and focus more on improving accuracy.

Increase the Distance Between You and Your Opponent

According to the formula *time = distance/velocity*, it is evident that as distance increases, so does the time a receiving player has to plan

Very slow speed   ◯   ◯

Moderate speed   ◯   ◯

Very fast speed   ◯   ◯

Figure 13.2   As you increase speed, you are likely to decrease accuracy.

a return. Translated into practice, this information explains why increasing the distance between the defender and the opponent when guarding fast-moving opponents can increase the time available to your defending athletes for a response. In tennis you will notice that most players stand farther back when expecting fast serves; the extra distance gives them more time to react to the ball and enables them to pick up directional cues later in the ball's flight.

You can use the same form of analysis for all sports in which an athlete has to react to the stimuli. It is the reason why a fastball in baseball and the flat serve in tennis are both so effective. When these and similar skills are performed effectively, the stimulus (i.e., ball or some other moving object) moves so fast (e.g., a volleyball spike) and for such a short distance that response time is extremely limited. In these instances athletes must learn to anticipate where the ball will be and when it will be there.

Learn to Anticipate

Several years ago Kane (1969) published the measured reaction time of the great heavyweight boxer Muhammed Ali responding to a

flashing light. His reaction time was about 190 milliseconds, which is about average. How long does a fist take to move 20 inches to hit an opponent? It takes a fast puncher about 40 milliseconds. As such, it is impossible for anyone to react fast enough to avoid the punch, so how was Ali able to avoid punches so well? The answer is *anticipation*. Ali was able to anticipate both the type of punch his opponent was going to throw and when he was going to throw it; he would start to move away well before his opponent's fist started to move toward him. If an athlete can predict which movement will be needed and when it will be needed, he or she will be able to prepare the response well before the stimulus occurs and overcome the usual reaction-time delays. In our tennis example, anticipation would give the player more time to return the shot, thereby enabling her to use the full backswing.

Let's consider another tennis example. Debbi has been watching her partner volley the tennis ball into the net, and volleying has continued to be the weakest part of Phil's game. Despite long hours of practice, the problem has not been corrected. Debbi thinks that Phil holds the racquet incorrectly. He has tried various grips but is still unable to volley effectively. What other errors might he be making?

As you probably anticipated, anticipation may be the key to Phil's problem. If Phil waits to decide to volley until the moment the ball leaves the opponent's racquet—that is, when the stimulus occurs—he does not have time to get into correct position to make the shot. Effective volleyers anticipate the shot well before the stimulus occurs. Phil, on the other hand, depends on Debbi to make the correct approach shot, and if it is not deep and towards center court, the return may be very difficult to volley regardless of how well it is anticipated. In contrast, when Debbi returns the ball, Phil must learn both to anticipate her shot and to move to the correct position on the court to cut off the opponent's return.

The relay exchange in swimming also exemplifies the importance of anticipation. The rules of swimming state that a swimmer must not leave the side of the pool before the incoming swimmer touches it. However, the rules do not prevent the waiting swimmer from starting to move before the incoming swimmer touches the side. If you teach your swimmers to start with their arms leaning forward, it takes several tenths of a second to swing them back, swing them forward, and then get the legs ready to push off the side of the pool to begin the dive. Thus, faster exchanges will occur if your swimmers start their movement while the incoming swimmer is approaching. Anticipating the incoming swimmer's touch is one key to getting faster relay times.

FACTORS INFLUENCING REACTION TIME

Many factors can influence the speed with which your athletes can react. In this section you will learn about some of the more important ones affecting reaction time.

Type of Stimulus

Your athletes will not react to various types of stimuli with the same speed; their reaction time will vary according to the sensory system receiving the stimulus, as shown in Figure 13.3.

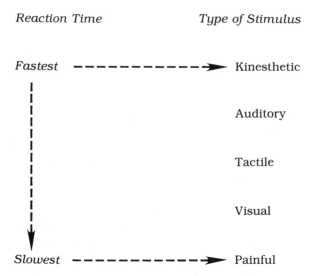

Figure 13.3 Reaction time varies with different types of stimuli.

For example, you can expect your athletes to react faster to a kinesthetic stimulus than to an auditory stimulus; likewise, they will respond faster to an auditory stimulus than to a visual stimulus.

Cue to Get Ready

A cue or warning signal alerting the athlete to react, like the one shown in Figure 13.1, will have an effect on your athlete's reaction time. You can expect that the reaction time of your athletes will be faster and less variable when a stimulus is preceded by such a cue or warning signal than when it is not. This is one reason why the starters of track and swimming races give the athletes a cue to get ready or set for the signal to start the race; they know that the athletes' reaction times will be faster and less variable when such a warning cue is given.

Foreperiod

The foreperiod, or time between the cue to get ready and the onset of the stimulus (see Figure 13.1), will have an effect on your athletes' reaction time. In fact, you can expect their reaction time to be a function of the number and the duration of different foreperiods used.

The greater the number of different foreperiods used, the more difficult it is to anticipate when the stimulus will occur. For example, a foreperiod in football is the time from when the quarterback sets up over the center until he calls out the count telling the center to snap the ball. A quarterbak who varies the start of plays by using five different center-snap counts makes it more difficult for the defense to anticipate when the play will begin than a quarterback who uses two counts. This assumes, of course, that none of the five counts is used more often by the quarterback than any of the others. If it is—and if the defense recognizes this tendency—they will learn to react to it more quickly than the other counts that are used less often.

If a quarterback uses a constant or nearly constant foreperiod play after play, the defense will learn to anticipate the snap of the ball and, like the offense, they will be able to respond exactly when the ball is snapped. By anticipating, the defense avoids the typical reaction-time delay that results if they wait until the ball is snapped to begin their response.

Your athletes' reaction time is also a function of the duration of the foreperiod immediately preceding it. For instance, suppose a quarterback uses a long count to start an offensive play. If he uses a short count to start the next play, the defense is likely to be surprised and thus react more slowly than if a long count followed a short one.

Obviously, quarterbacks vary the count (foreperiod) to prevent the defense from anticipating when the football will be snapped, but football is not the only sport utilizing this strategy. For example, starters of track and swimming races, already mentioned, also attempt to prevent athletes from anticipating the start by deliberately varying the foreperiod; that is, they vary the amount of time between the cue to get ready to start the race and firing the pistol to signal the start of the race.

Intensity of Stimulus

Within some limits, the intensity (strength) of the stimulus will influence your athletes' reaction time. The stronger the stimulus, the faster the reaction time up to a point. A slight increase in stimulus strength at low-stimulus intensities produces a considerable difference in reaction time, but proportionally less effect occurs as the stimulus intensity is increased. This information has been useful, for example, in sprint races in track and swimming: It has been determined that the athlete closest to the starter at the beginning of the race has a slightly faster reaction time than the athlete who is farthest away because the closer you are to the starting pistol, the louder it sounds. The athlete closest to the starter has a slight advantage at the start of the race, and although it may be only a few milliseconds, it may be enough to win the race. To avoid this inequity in national and international competitions, the start of a race is signaled by a sound stimulus presented to each athlete at a constant intensity and located at the same distance from each athlete, and no one gains an unfair reaction-time advantage.

Time Between Successive Stimuli

If, for example, two stimuli are presented and the time between them ranges from about 50 to 250 milliseconds, it will take longer to react to the second stimulus than to the first. When a receiver fakes running deep for a pass (first stimulus) and then stops suddenly (second

stimulus) about 50 to 250 milliseconds after the fake, and begins running back towards the quarterback to receive the pass, the defensive back's reaction time to the sudden stop will be slower than it was to the fake, causing considerable disadvantage. This effect clearly points out the importance of properly spacing the time between the fake to set up the opponent and the move made after the fake. The proper timing between fake and move is definitely worth practicing to get a jump on the opponent. Begin by experimenting with the timing of fakes. Once you determine what works best for your athletes, encourage them to practice at competitive speed to perfect their timing.

Number of Stimuli

Reaction time will be affected if your athletes have to make choices such as which stimulus requires a response or which response is best, given a certain stimulus. Reaction time becomes slower as the number of alternative stimuli and responses increases. For example, suppose you are wrestling an opponent who effectively uses four different takedowns. Furthermore, assume that each of the four takedowns requires you to execute a different counterresponse to prevent being taken down. You do not know which of four possible takedowns (stimuli) your opponent will try or how you will have to react. Your problem is also complicated by not knowing when the takedown attempt will take place.

Compare this wrestling situation with one in which your opponent has two different takedowns, each requiring a different countermove. Would you be able to react faster in the four-takedown situation or in the two-takedown situation? The answer is obvious: Reaction time against the two-takedown opponent will be faster. The same would be true if you compared a two-takedown situation with a one-takedown situation. You would react even faster in a one-takedown situation that required only one countermove response.

Concentration During the Foreperiod

Consider situations such as track or swimming races involving one stimulus and one response. You can expect your athletes to react faster to the stimulus to begin the race if they concentrate during the foreperiod on the stimulus rather than on the movement to be made in response to it (assuming that the response is well learned and the athlete does not have to think to execute it). When the starter gives the cue to get ready to start the race, the athlete should concentrate on hearing the sound of the starter's pistol being fired, not on the movements that have to be made to get out of the blocks and begin the race.

Practice

Practice will make reaction time slightly faster, but you can expect the greatest improvement to occur over the first few practices. Although reaction time may continue to improve with subsequent practice, the improvement is likely to be very small. Movement time, on the other hand, can be greatly improved with practice. In fact, compared to reaction time, movement time will improve much more as a function of practice, largely as the result of improved skill technique and/or physical conditioning.

Condition and Age of Athletes

The physical, cognitive, and motivational condition of your athletes at the moment they must react to a stimulus will affect their reaction time. Their reactions will be slowed by very strenuous exercise demands on their physical state, very high information processing demands on their mental state, and/or a lack of motivation. You can also expect their reaction times to get faster as they get older, up to about 19 years of age. From this point to about 25 years of age will be their fastest and reaction time should be at its peak.

HELPING YOUR ATHLETES TO ANTICIPATE

Many factors will significantly influence your athletes' ability to anticipate, and you need to know what they are and how they operate if

you are to be able to help them. Let's examine in more detail the influence of some of these factors on anticipation.

Knowing When an Event Will Happen

Knowing *when* an event will occur is a major concern in situations where an athlete knows in advance *what* response to make. With a track response like the sprint start, the time it takes an athlete to react is known as *simple reaction time*—the time from the onset of the starting signal to the initiation of the response. All the information needed to perform the response is known before the starting signal occurs, and the athlete does not have to make any response choices. The athlete knows the movement response that must follow the starting signal; he or she also knows that the movement must begin immediately after the firing of the starter's pistol. In these situations the only way an athlete can shorten reaction time is to anticipate when the pistol will be fired. To help their athletes, experienced track coaches often tell them to listen to the start of all the races before their own race to see if they can detect a regular or predictable temporal pattern in the way the starter begins each race. However, experienced starters deliberately do not use the same time periods (foreperiods) between *ready* and *go* signals to try to prevent athletes from gaining an unfair advantage from anticipation. The starters hope that all the athletes will react to, rather than anticipate, the gunshot and start at approximately the same time.

Knowing What Event Will Happen

Will the next pitch be a fastball or a curve? Will the quarterback throw long or short? Will the basketball player leading the fastbreak pass or shoot? If you are uncertain about which event is to occur, you will have more difficulty anticipating your response. Athletes must often contend with uncertainties about how and when an event will take place. For example, if a certain player always takes the free kick in soccer, the opposition can learn how to defend against it. If, however, the player fakes the play and lets someone else take the kick once or twice in a match, the opposition will be poorly prepared for the timing and execution.

In most sports you can teach athletes cues to help them anticipate certain events. For example, when facing a right-handed baseball pitcher, the runner at first base should look at the pitcher's right heel at the beginning of the wind up. If the heel is lifted, the runner is forewarned that the pitcher is going to throw to first base to try a pickoff. The heel staying down tells the runner that the pitcher will throw to the batter. In either case, the runner will be able to anticipate what the pitcher will do by focusing on the pitcher's right heel, enabling the runner to prepare a response before the pitcher throws the ball. When teaching, think about key cues that will help your athletes anticipate plays.

Being Prepared for Likely Events

The more plays your athletes must contend with, the more difficulty they will have anticipating the next play. Under these circumstances, what can you do to prepare your athletes? One answer is to prepare them for the most likely events. Your opponents will almost certainly use some plays more often

than others in specific situations. By studying or scouting them ahead of time and determining what their tendencies are, you can tell your athletes what to expect.

While you are looking for predictable response patterns among your opponents, you can be sure that they will be interested in the predictability of your athletes. Therefore, take care to avoid becoming too predictable. For example, if you are coaching football and use a lot of plays but tend to use the same plays in certain situations, the opposition will find it easy to make the correct defensive adjustments. Instead of being too predictable, you should occasionally utilize the unexpected. Can you think of instances in your sport when you can use a play or move that will surprise the opposition?

If a move or play works, you may be tempted to try the same move again, but unless you are convinced that the opposition has been fooled into believing that you will not try the same play again, it may be unwise to repeat the play. For example, the baseline return shot is a relatively safe shot in tennis. Attacking this shot becomes very easy if a player uses it on consecutive rallies and does not vary play with different types of shots.

The same holds true for most sports. Not only must your athletes be capable of varying their strategy, but they must learn to introduce variety into their performance. If your middle-distance runners always race the same way, opponents quickly learn an effective counterstrategy. Staying in second or third position until the final turn and then kicking for the finish line may be the easiest way to run a race, but it is also the most predictable: The strategy is too easy to anticipate. The best athletes not only possess excellent physical skills, but they also know—in part because of their coaches' efforts—how to outthink their opponents.

Signaling Movements

Athletes react faster to signals that are clear and distinct from other signals. You must teach your athletes how to communicate clearly with teammates as well as how to disguise their signals from opponents. When methods of signaling are well known and easily observable (e.g. verbal messages, hand signals, and body movements) your task is to disguise the meaning so that opponents do not have time to plan a response in advance of the impending event. The challenge is to select signals that do not confuse your own athletes and yet cannot be easily detected by opponents.

Uncertainty can be increased in some sports by disguising the skill itself. For example, coaches of racquet sports encourage their players to make all the initial movements of each shot look as similar as possible. Players learn to wait until later in the pattern to alter their movement for a specific shot. The two-handed backhand in tennis, a shot that has experienced widespread popularity in recent years, is especially effective because it enables the player to disguise the direction of the shot until the last moment, giving opponents much less time to anticipate the shot and plan their return.

Finding the Right Player at the Right Time

Some athletes are very effective players partly because they make passes to players who are in the best position to make the desired plays. This is one of the reasons that basketball player Larry Bird and ice hockey forward Wayne Gretzky are such valuable players. They can find the right player at the right time. Sports writer Tom Callahan points out that players of this caliber

see and play the game several moves ahead of the moment, comprehending not only where everything is but also where everything will be. Shown a photograph of a nondescript instant on the ice, Gretzky can replace the unpictured performers here and there about the periphery and usually recall what became of them the next second (1985, p. 52).

Making the right choices at the right time depends to a marked degree upon your athletes' ability to anticipate. Some athletes seem naturally to develop their ability to anticipate, whereas others need to be taught. For example, Coach Kathy Smith was concerned that her basketball team's field goal percentage was lower this season than last year and started to think about the playing qualities of

Larry Bird and Wayne Gretzky. She recalled the main difference between her team this year and last year was that her best guard had graduated. Although all her other players had returned, each one was shooting below last year's percentage. After careful observation Kathy decided that her players were not taking shots from their best positions on the court, and this factor was lowering shooting percentage. The players were not finding the best player on the court to pass to on their own and did not know how to change this. Kathy had never thought about teaching her players how to find teammates in their best positions but finally decided that if her guards were not finding players naturally, she would try to teach them. She videotaped her athletes in action. Her information feedback while watching the video focused on finding the right player in the best positions. During a team meeting she asked the players when and to whom they should have passed, based on their respective positions on the court and each athlete's strengths. At the next practice, after the players understood what she wanted them to do, she positioned them on the court in various game situations and had them practice trying to find the right player at the right time. Before long, she found that her guards' court awareness and anticipation had improved dramatically. Both guards were looking for players who could shoot consistently from the position they were in. After a few games all her players had improved their shooting percentages. If you coach a team sport, consider how you might improve the ability of your athletes to find the right player at the right time.

SUMMARY AND RECOMMENDATIONS

Contrary to popular opinion, fast responses in sport do not depend as much on reflexes—involuntary, innate responses to stimuli—as they do on fast reactions and movements that are voluntary, learned responses to stimuli. Understanding the speed of voluntary responses and which factors affect them is critical to helping your athletes overcome slow reactions and/or slow movements. The following summary and recommendations will help you teach your athletes how to improve both reaction time and speed of movements.

1. Reaction time plus movement time equals response time. A foreperiod usually precedes a reaction time.

   • Foreperiod is the time from the cue to get ready to the onset of the stimulus.

   • Reaction time is the time from the onset of the stimulus to the initiation of the movement.

   • Movement time is the time from initiation of the movement until its completion.

2. Some of the factors that influence reaction time are as follows:

   • The type of stimulus producing the fastest reaction time has been found to come in this order: kinesthetic, auditory, tactile, visual, and painful.

   • Reaction time is faster and less variable when a stimulus is preceded by a cue to get ready than when it is not.

   • Reaction time is slower when reacting to more foreperiods of variable length (up to a point) and when a short foreperiod follows a long one.

   • Within limits, reaction time becomes faster as the intensity of the stimulus increases.

   • When two stimuli occur within 50-250 milliseconds of each other, it takes longer to react to the second stimulus than to the first.

   • Reaction time becomes slower (up to a point) as an increase occurs in the number of response choices and/or the variety of response choices.

   • Reaction time can become slightly faster with practice, whereas movement time can become dramatically improved with practice.

   • Reaction time is slowed by very high physical and/or cognitive demands; it is also slowed by a lack of motivation to perform.

   • Reaction time gets faster as an athlete's age increases and is fastest between the ages of 19 and 25.

3. You can help your athletes overcome slow responses by having them

   • Shorten their movement time by shortening the distance of their movements when the average velocity of the movements is held constant;

   • Move faster—but remember the speed-accuracy tradeoff: as they increase the speed of their movements, accuracy decreases; as they increase the accuracy of their movements, speed decreases;

   • Learn to anticipate the appropriate response and when to use it so that your athletes will be able to prepare their response well before the stimulus occurs and thus avoid the usual reaction-time delay. Teach them to look for opponents' regularities, predictable tendencies, and cues.

Conclusions

We'd like to conclude this book by emphasizing the need for individualizing your coaching and teaching. We've provided you with so much information, given you so many principles and procedures, and made so many recommendations that it's easy to forget you will be dealing with many different individuals at different levels of development. What works successfully with one athlete may fail with another. There's no sure bet when teaching athletes new sport skills. However, what we have tried to do in this book is to bring together the findings of researchers and practitioners so that the challenge you face is a bit more manageable. Some final messages and thoughts follow that will help you to individualize your coaching and teaching.

When you are coaching try to keep in mind that readiness for learning a sport or a particular sport skill depends not only on a youngster's motivation, but also on his or her level of development. The level an athlete will reach at a particular chronological age will depend on the combined influences of heredity and environment. Heredity will provide the basic potential for the young athlete's development, but the appropriate environmental experiences will be needed for it to be realized. An athlete's level of development mainly depends on three factors:

- prior environmental experiences including his or her background of previously learned skills;
- the traits with which he or she is hereditarily endowed; and
- the rate at which these traits unfold, that is, his or her maturation rate.

All of your young athletes will tend to follow a predictable pattern of development that proceeds progressively from the simple to the complex. However, the rate of development will differ considerably among your athletes, which is one reason why all of them may not be ready to learn the same sport skills at the same age. The implication for coaching is that instruction should be individualized as much as possible. This can be done by planning for the skills to be learned and the expectancies concerning the performance in relation to each athlete's level of development. Such planning will enable you to provide the opportunity for each of your athletes to experience a reasonable degree of success throughout the learning process. This planning will also enable you to avoid situations in which your athletes experience repeated failure in trying to learn sport skills for which they are not ready. Such situations should be avoided because they are likely to have a detrimental effect on your athletes' development.

Although a youngster should not be expected to learn a sport or sport skill before he or she is developmentally ready, some sports and skills can be introduced by modifying such things as the rules of the game and/or the equipment and facilities used to play the sport or perform the skill. Some examples of such modifications currently in use are (a) shorter time periods in youth wrestling and soccer, and six innings instead of nine innings in Little League Baseball; (b) smaller and lighter soccer balls, basketballs, and baseballs, (c) lower basketball baskets; (d) reduced dimensions for basketball courts, soccer and baseball fields, and (e) scaled down versions of skis, tennis racquets, baseball bats, and gymnastics equipment. We are not saying that it is advisable to have your athletes learn any sport or sport skill simply because it can be modified. You must first judge whether the sport or skill you want your athletes to learn will be more beneficial than harmful to their emotional, physical, social, and/or intellectual development. If you think it will be more beneficial, then go ahead and modify the rules of the game, the equipment, or the facilities. This will enable your athletes to learn what you want them to learn and will contribute to their development.

If you coach young athletes, do remember

that early performance successes do not necessarily predict later successes. Conversely, failures or early learning difficulties are poor indicators of a youngster's potential. As athletes grow and develop, their bodies change in size and shape. These changes are accompanied by unpredictable changes in ability. Many children who excel as youngsters do not excel as they get older. In contrast, it is not uncommon for a child who experiences learning difficulties early on, but who remains interested in sport, to later blossom into an outstanding athlete. Prepare your athletes for these changes by trying to give equal attention to each regardless of playing ability.

Finally, we encourage you to think carefully about the role each athlete plays on your team. Perhaps he or she has a special ability that is ideally suited for one particular playing position. Beware, however, of encouraging specialization with younger athletes; they will enjoy the greatest benefit from early exposure to a variety of sport experiences. Above all remember that it is the interaction with you, the learning of new skills, having fun, and making new friends that will make participation in your sport program a winning experience for everyone.

REFERENCES

American Optometric Association. (n.d). *You can't hit it if you can't see it.* St. Louis: Author.

Callahan, T. (1985, March 18). Masters of their own game. *Time,* p. 5.

Fischman, M. G., Christina, R.W., & Vercruyssen, M.J. (1982). Retention and transfer of motor skills. *Quest, 33,* 181–194.

Fitts, P. M. (1954). The information capacity of the human motor system in controlling the amplitude of movement. *Journal of Experimental Psychology, 47,* 381–391.

Gallwey, W. T. (1974). *The inner game of tennis.* New York: Random House.

Judd, C. H. (1908). The relation of special training to general intelligence. *Educational Review, 36,* 28–42.

Kane, M. (1969, May 5). The art of Ali. *Sports Illustrated,* pp. 48–57.

Kottke, F. J., Halpern, D., Easton, J. K., Ozel, A. T., & Burrill, B. S. (1978). The training of coordination. *Archives of Physical Medicine and Rehabilitation Medicine, 59,* 567–572.

Landers, D.M., & Daniels, F.S. (1983). Understanding physical development. In R. Martens, R. W. Christina, J. S. Harvey, Jr., & B. J. Sharkey (Eds.), *Coaching young athletes* (NRA ed.). pp. 119-123. Champaign, IL: Human Kinetics.

Martens, R. (1987). *Coaches guide to sport psychology.* Champaign, IL: Human Kinetics.

Martens, R., Christina, R. W., Harvey, J. S., Jr., & Sharkey, B. J. (1981). *Coaching young athletes.* Champaign, IL: Human Kinetics.

Martens, R. & Seefeldt, V. (1979). *Guidelines for children's sports.* Washington, DC: AAHPERD.

Mehrabian, A. (1976, August). The three dimensions of emotional reaction. *Psychology Today,* pp. 59-60, 114.

Nicklaus, J., & Bowden, K. (1974). *Golf my way.* New York: Simon & Schuster.

Nideffer, R. M. (1985). *Athlete's guide to mental training.* Champaign, IL: Human Kinetics.

Oxendine, J. B. (1970). Emotional arousal and motor performance. *Quest, 13,* 23–32.

Sharkey, B. J. (1986). *Coaches guide to sport physiology.* Champaign, IL: Human Kinetics.

Singer, R. N. (1980). *Motor learning and human performance.* New York: Macmillan.

Thomas, J. R., Thomas, K. T., & Gallagher, J. D. (1984). Children's processing of information in physical activity and sport. In J. R. Thomas (Ed.), *Children's motor skill development: Motor development during childhood and adolescence.* Minneapolis: Burgess.

Wiren, G. (1968). Teaching golf: How is your approach? *The Physical Educator, 25,* 51–53.

SUPPLEMENTARY REFERENCES

Cratty, B. J. (1973). *Movement behavior and motor learning* (3rd ed.). Philadelphia: Lea & Febiger.

Fitts, P. M. (1964). Perceptual-motor skill learning. In A. Melton (Ed.), *Categories of human learning,* New York: Academic Press.

Fitts, P. M., & Posner, M. I. (1967). *Human performance.* Belmont, CA: Brooks/Cole.

Gould, D. R., & Roberts, G. C. (1982). Modeling and motor skill acquisition. *Quest, 33,* 214–230.

Kerr, R. (1982). *Psychomotor learning.* New York: Saunders College Publishing.

Kleinman, M. (1983). *The acquisition of motor skill.* Princeton, NJ: Princeton Book Co.

Landers, D. M. (1978). How, when, and where to use demonstrations: Suggestions for the practitioner. *Journal of Physical Education and Recreation,* **49**, 65–67.

Lawther, J. D. (1977). The learning and performance of physical skills (2nd ed.). Englewood Cliffs, NJ: Prentice-Hall.

Magill, R. A. (1985). *Motor learning: concept and applications* (2nd ed.). Dubuque, IA: Wm. C. Brown.

Marteniuk, R. G. (1976). *Information processing in motor skills.* New York: Holt, Rinehart, and Winston.

Oxendine, J. B. (1984). *Psychology of motor learning* (2nd ed.). Englewood Cliffs, NJ: Prentice-Hall.

Rushall, B. S., & Siedentop, D. (1972). *The development and control of behavior in sport and physical education.* Philadelphia: Lea & Febiger.

Sabock, R. J. (1985). *The coach* (3rd ed.). Champaign, IL: Human Kinetics.

Sage, G. H. (1984). *Motor learning and control: A neuropsychological approach.* Dubuque, IA: Wm. C. Brown.

Schmidt, R. A. (1982). *Motor control and learning.* Champaign, IL: Human Kinetics.

Singer, R. N., & Dick, W. (1980). *Teaching physical education: A systems approach.* Boston: Houghton Mifflin.

Stallings, L. M. (1982). *Motor learning from theory to practice.* St. Louis: C. V. Mosby.

Weinberg, R. S. (1982). The relationship between mental preparation strategies and motor performance: A review and critique. *Quest,* **33**, 195–213.

Index

Mechanical principles, 34–35, 81
Mehrabian, A., 134
Memory, 121–127
  and forgetting, 122, 123, 124, 125
  and knowledge errors, 121, 122, 127
  long-term, 121–127
  and motor programs, 122, 123
  and movement errors, 121–122, 127
  short-term, 121–127
  stages of, 122–123
  ways to improve, 126–127
Methods of teaching, 75–82. *See also* Difficult
  skills
  backward chaining, 76–78, 82
  part, 56, 57, 75, 82
  part-whole, 76
  progressive-part, 76
  repetitive part, 77
  selection of, 78–79
  whole-part-whole, 77
Modifying skills, 95–96, 97
Motivation, 42–43, 85, 86, 93, 94, 97, 105,
  106, 107
Motor ability, 22, 24–25
Motor program, 20–21, 22, 24, 25, 26, 27, 122,
  123
Movement time, 137, 138, 143, 146

N icole

Nicklaus, J., 116
Nideffer, R., 135

O

Open skills, 130, 131. *See also* Difficult skills;
  Method of teaching; Part method

P

Plateaus, 70–72, 73
  causes of, 70–71
  defined, 70
  and practice, 70–71
  solutions for, 71–72
Practice, 63–73
  distributed, 64, 66, 67, 72
  duration of, 67
  and errors, 69, 70
  fatigued conditions, 68, 72
  frequency of, 63, 64, 65–66, 67
  imagery, 115, 116
  intensity of, 67
  intentions, 65
  length of, 63, 64
  massed, 64, 65
  mental, 63, 113, 118

  and overpractice, 67–68, 73
  and performance objectives, 11–13, 17
  plan, 13
  principles of, 13–14
  and reminiscence, 66
  for speed vs. accuracy, 69, 73
Punishment. *See* Feedback

R

Reaction time, 137–146
  and age, 143, 146
  and concentration, 142–143, 146
  and condition, 143, 146
  defined, 146
  and foreperiod, 141–142, 146
  and interstimulus interval, 142, 146
  and number of stimuli, 142, 146
  and practice, 143, 146
  and stimulus intensity, 142, 146
  and type of stimulus, 141, 146
  and warning signal, 141, 146
Reinforcement. *See* Feedback
Response time, 137, 138, 146

S

Seefeldt, V., 64
Self-confidence, 22, 24, 25, 26
Shaping skills, 94–95, 97
Sharkey, B., 3, 13, 14, 61
Slow responses, 138–141
Speed-accuracy tradeoff, 139

T

Thomas, J., 126
Thomas, K., 126
Transfer of learning, 34, 35, 79–82, 102, 109
  bilateral, 81–82
  defined, 79
  and mechanical principles, 81
  negative, 80, 106
  and new skills, 20
  positive, 79, 106
  and skill similarity, 80, 81, 82
  and specificity of practice, 82
  teaching for, 79–82
  zero, 80

V

Vercruyssen, M., 82

W

Warm-up, 13
Whole method. *See* Difficult skills; Methods of
  teaching
Wiren, G., 101